THE WAYS TO WIT

Joshua Smith

Printed in the United States of America

Never seem wiser, nor more learned, than the people you are with. Wear your learning like your watch, in a private pocket: and do not pull it out and strike it; merely to show that you have one. If you are asked what o'clock it is, tell it; but do not proclaim it hourly and unasked, like the watchman.

-Philip Stanhope, 4th Earl of Chesterfield

Table of Contents

Wit

A DIAGNOSIS

Whilst John the Carpenter lies sleeping atop his medieval roof in night's darkness, waiting for the second diluvial flood in a tethered-down bathtub, his adulterous wife, Alisoun, is sticking her medieval rump out of a window for the rich and culturally learned parish cleric Absolon to kiss. After his lips connect with her beard, and therefrom learning that he had not kissed her face, Absolon shows discontent and demands redemption. A second attempt is awarded. And, this time, he puckers blindly up for the even more formidable nether region of Alisoun's paramour, Nicholas, who, when the parish leader's face enters proximity, encourages forth a honking gust, whereupon Absolon modifies Nicholas's hind parts by way of scorching hot plow blade. Nicholas howls, as John, still in the aforementioned bathtub, comes crashing through the roof and into the marital bedroom.

A few years or so later, Sir John Falstaff's heap of flesh is red in the face, breathing heavily, and shouting at young Hal, Prince of Wales and heir to the throne of England, to grab him a cup of sack. From there, Falstaff recounts to the den of thieves before him last night's highway robbery and subsequent triumph over a hundred, a dozen, sixteen, twenty-three, or, perhaps, fifty opponents, two of whom, nay, four, seven, nine—indeed—eleven were clad in buckram suits. Falstaff's armor peppered with perforations, his sword after the shape of a hacksaw hacked, Hal's suspicions are piqued. This doubt is bolstered by Falstaff's notoriety as a coward and liar. Misgivings increase still for Hal, for it was he himself who was that same man cloaked at the Witching Hour who persuaded Falstaff away from his booty by taking it for his own, leaving Falstaff to scamper away in so gutless a manner as to contradict how a man with such a gut should be able to scamper. Falstaff is then, not for the last time, called out for his mendacity and, by his only friends, openly humiliated and shamed. Falstaff, however, chops logic accordingly, acquitting himself of any moral tomfoolery, and thence finding a suitable haystack to rest his unaffected girth.

These are the foundations of English literature. Of course, these are Chaucer's and Shakespeare's creations, respectively. And, although Chaucer and Shakespeare are rather sizable columns indeed in the architecture of English literature, it was their gift and keen eye for wit and humor that remain steadfast as the foundations of the English-speaking mind.

To write on the topics of Wit and Humor, however, is a near contradiction in itself: they are paradoxes of ever-revolving relations; they exist by being nothing and disappear by becoming something; they serve as both the journey and the destination. To arrive at laughter, there are many ways to wit, and one must walk them all at once, in order to feign arrival.

Wit is, however, not taught in schools and is not any part of any formal study thereafter. It is not even a word much a part of conversation anymore, nor, whenever a part of conversation, used intelligibly. Nevertheless, wit is an experience definitely recognizable by its creators and audiences alike.

Quick and innovating thinking resulting in the creation of an original synthesis of likenesses between notions and knowledge might prick up a few ears. This creation depends not on the logical connection of closely related material, rather on the spontaneous copulation of ideas leading to the birth of some arcane association binding the familiar and the unfamiliar, coalescing from the memory seemingly discrete concepts or images that call upon the imagination to blend the dimensions of the physical and the literal with the metaphorical and the allegorical. And, should this lead to a humorous effect, then all the greater slap on the back.

Or, as a sort of pillage and burn definition, wit is a form of verbal calculus, the ultimate test of which is the ability to balance intelligence with wisdom in the interest of discovering novel patterns of imagery that tickle the brain, curl the lip, and, in short, make life worth living.

In witty writing, intelligence is the sharp, linguistic dexterity—the grammatical prowess, narrative constructions, and rhetorical schemes that strike one as inherently clever, stroking the part of the brain responsible for pattern recognition. Wisdom is the deeper metaphorical and ironic tropes that divine new imagery innate to wit's brilliant kind of associative thinking. To render these separate senses upon the page as one seamless formation is to render the quintessence of the subject of this book.

What, then, is the first step required to activate the aforementioned quintessence?

Chess over checkers, boxing over brawling, math over monkey-brains: indeed, one of the most impressive phenomena to observe is deliberateness; and, at the core of any instance of wit, there is deliberateness. Whenever we experience deliberateness, we want to know what it means, how it was done, and how we as sub-human homunculi can become more deliberate ourselves. Thankfully, creating deliberate, witty patterns in one's writing is as simple as knowing the correct formulas for one's readership to appreciably decipher. And the best way to learn the correct formulas is to imbibe liberally from the masters of them.

From Shakespeare to Samuel Johnson, from Seinfeld to Simon Pegg, there are, throughout the history of the English language, a goodish many fountains of wit from which one my choose to slake one's smirk-thirst. Books upon books could be written about Shakespeare's contributions to wit—and have been. Therefore, The Bard's donations shall, in this volume, remain unmolested. Samuel Johnson's is a formidable mind on the topic and thus will be left to better scholars with greater supplies of Excedrin Latinate. Benjamin Franklin, George Costanza, Johnathan Swift, Winston Churchill, Abraham Lincoln, C.S. Lewis, Chael Sonnen: all admirable Wits. None of them a topic in this book.

The aim of this book is to provide a substitute for pistol and ball. Moreover, it is to put on display ten of the most brilliant Wits of modern literary history; that is, ten of the most brilliant professional "prose" writers who got their start during or after the Industrial Revolution. The gentlemen of this volume founded entire careers, entire lives, indeed immortalized themselves by writing the very best wit that English-reading eyes have the ability to encounter. They are the authors who have not only taught all those after them how to read, write, and think truly wittily, but who have also been the role-models and paragons for all writers interested in turning a grinning phrase that leaves readers sounding like a retired Clydesdale choking on the fumes of a cheap cigar.

Although each of these gentlemen have more of the wild-goose in one of his wits than, I am sure, I have in my whole five, I have nonetheless taken the liberty of diagnosing the syndrome of a finely written wit through the observation of five main symptoms:

Firstly, the affected will develop a clinical *anxiety* about language. A punctilious attitude towards the foundations of language inevitably leads to an interconnected texture of painstaking deliberateness. Just as employing the utmost skill with one's grammar and lexicon displays masterful control, a fastidious attention to exact usage ensures that sentence-logic will be water-tight and wordplay of the first water. An utter rejection of cliche phrasing whilst creating linguistic patterns is a necessity. And all good writing, and one might go as far as saying everything that has ever gone well at all, has good transitions. To toss one ball in the air and then to do it again with another ball, and still another ball, is a task for an ape in a patterned tie. To perform the same feat as one catches the last ball and transitions it to the other hand, whilst a third ball flies skyward, begins to appear majestic. Likewise, transition from one idea to another with sophistication and readers begin to revere its architect as one who could probably fix a problem without repeatedly stopping to pull his up pants.

Thereafter, an *obsession* with the rhetorical can be observed. The topic of rhetorical forms is vast and possesses great heft; therefore, I concern myself here chiefly with the rhetorical forms called schemes, which improve the quality of sentence-length turn of phrase. But not with just any old rhetorical scheme. The rhetorical schemes mastered by the immortals herein depicted have been combed for the proper permutation of playfulness. They allow the intelligence to take over, organizing one's thoughts and notions into finely wrapped packages of sentence-length joy.

An *addiction* to creating new and creative images through the use of metaphor, simile, analogy, allegory, and other systems of associative thought typically follows. These rhetorical tropes portrayed by the following authors best allow associative thinking to take over, freeing one's mind to compare many things simultaneously and dream new comparisons to life, thus allowing one's wisdom to be at play. Much like a pun of words, image-puns show a great truth by saying two, three, indeed an infinite number of things at once.

In advanced stages, a *compulsion* towards juxtaposing narrative forms manifests. There are nowadays heaps of narrative threads available to dress one's work up into any sort of parlor trick. This symptom is concerned, however, with the narrative forms used by these master Wits that make one's writing not edgy, confusing, or obscure, rather wittier. It is concerned with a narrative's speed, interconnectedness, and employment of meaningfully humorous juxtapositions.

Finally, an ironic tone leaves the writer incapable of constructing a sentence that simply conveys information, rendering him *hopeless*. If successful, the Wit's inability to speak plainly should infect all parts of his life. Irony levels may be measured through the writer's deliberate contrast between subject matter and its treatment. The affected will grow a second tongue, such that the original says one thing above, whilst the second says something else below. This can be, at times, difficult to observe, as it is a subtle symptom that must betray meaning without too obviously doing so. Whenever irony has metastasized, writers will conflict form and content in such a manner that, were the two in harmony, they could not be expressed half so well.

All together, these are sure to make a most sharp sauce.

Within these pages is by no means an exhaustive delineation of all concepts of wit. Each of the Wits presented herein, however, has his trademarks, the tools of his trade manifesting differently. Some are famous for farce or humorous imagery, some for darkly ironic description and rhetorical flourish, whilst others chop words to etymological bits and allude to the history of literature. It must be stated, however, that each of these Wits can perform the other's trademarks with not only tantamount ability, but also, perhaps, do so with even more skill for which the other is illustrious. Thus, through the following showcase of some of the greatest humorists that English literature has ever known, may we also learn the ways to wit._

P.G. Wodehouse

THE TRUTH ABOUT LOOKING FUNNY

Any humorist worth his Serotonin Reuptake Inhibitors is not only fluent in many languages, but he can also speak them all at once. He must know, at the native level, the language of every other art form to have a chance of not being taken seriously in his own. Comedy must know the dagger of tragedy, the demon or fear, the lurking figure of mystery. Should the humorist be not devastatingly learned in these genres, we might take him for some witless teller of jokes. And no one likes a joke—it is why we can never remember one. But what one never forgets are those Dionysian belly-laughs that redden knees, stand in for elite exercise, and suggest the imminence of pulmonary distress—enter Sir Pelham Grenville Wodehouse.

The eminent humorist P.G. Wodehouse is known for his crisp wit, inimitable lexical prowess, and above all, his staggering ability to leave readers fresh out of abdominal strength. Wodehouse's career as a writer spanned over 70 years. Why, then, with a list of titles as long as the body count in Camden, New Jersey, does each one surprise and tickle with a mirth hitherto unsurmised? Wodehouse was a prolific writer of farce, and his skills for leaving powerless readers examining their ribs for the quisling's bodkin is but the product of a complete mastery of craft. The great Evelyn Waugh hailed Wodehouse as "the head of my profession," and, although I am no worshipper of the late Rev. Christopher Hitchens, I cannot find his typical casuistry within his statement, "P.G. Wodehouse is the Gold Standard of English Wit."

Wodehouse's lighthearted books certainly have their leitmotifs. Love and limerence are never too far in the offing. Likewise, it would not be an altogether uncommon experience, whenever casting a glance over the Wodehouse canon, to witness a few lines about an engagement in jeopardy, a bobby's helmet purloined, or an aunt less than gruntled. Indeed, the wonderfully disappointing blessing that one receives by reading one Wodehouse story is that, when finished, one can find repose in knowing that he has read *every* Wodehouse story. Language, tone, plot: It's all the same. Moreover, there are but few, if any, true villains in Wodehouse's works. Yet, one has always been a close contender for the crown: The Artist.

Those committed to the grave endeavors of Art and Truth intensely dislike the men and women of Wit. Luckily, the feeling is reciprocated by the latter upon the former. As a general rule, it is never a bad idea, for the purposes of humor, to direct one's efforts rather strongly upon a few worthy and sporting opponents, as it brings forth a natural zest for the task at hand. It is paramount, however, that one employ, whilst in pursuit of properly maligning one's fellow contriver of aesthetic artifices, the very highest registers of art. Base commentary will be met with basic reactions, and rightly so. To insult someone precisely, though, is the highest form of respect, as it evinces a unique, deep-seated infatuation for the beloved unsurpassed by other simulacrums of affection.

Wodehouse is rather notorious for his lovingly mild critiques of poets, painters, and pretentious pains in the posterior of all kinds. In his 1917 novel, *Piccadilly Jim,* during a scene depicting a shindig inhabited by bohemians, this predilection for putting down his fellow "breed" is wisely unleashed.

He begins by batting around a few ameliorative depictions of those peace-loving wearers of berets we all know and love. Would it not be without some justifiably "strong objections," that the Wit's gentle philistine soul should enter a room quarantined by "the hoarse cries of futurist painters, esoteric Buddhists, *vers libre* poets, interior decorators and stage reformers...men with new religions...(and) women with new hats?" Can we not already envision, amongst this "jamboree" of the enlightened avant-garde, "Ernest Wisden, the playwright...Lora Delance Porter, the feminist writer...Clara What's-Her-Name, the sculptor, with the bobbed hair?" Is it not also common knowledge that, if one were to attend a party with "that mental broadening process already alluded to," that one should expect to be "pounced on by a woman who talked to him for an hour about the morality of finance and [who] seem(s) to think that millionaires (are) the scum of the earth"? Indeed, it is empirically sound to conclude that, when in the "environs" of such genius, great swathes of sheep-grazed shire will inevitably be "dominated...by an angular woman who (is) saying loud and penetrating things about the suffrage."

Tableaus of such evils are enough. Imagine, then, the traumatic experience of actually having to traverse such a beastly throng. To posit this extreme mental exercise as being equally reminiscent to "plung(ing) into a pack of wild coyotes" only to be "torn to pieces by wild poets" is no great stretch of the imagination. Therefore, in the simple interest of self-preservation, it is best for one to find a way around incurring such savage acts of mayhem and the subsequent bodily harm pursuant thereto. One way certain to preclude the aforementioned carnage would be to interpose upon the scene the spirited cries of a spoiled child being pummeled to crabmeat by a former professional boxer.

Wodehouse decides to employ in his narrative exactly that certainty, whereupon all "twelve highly intellectual topics" meet their instantaneous demise: "futurist painters stared pallidly as *vers libre* poets, speech smitten from their lips, and stage reformers looked at esoteric Buddhists with wild surmise." Yet, no good, mismatched street-fight is complete without a decent exploration of the conquered's abdominals with the steel toe of the victor's size-fifteen boot. And, it is with a lively kick indeed that Wodehouse describes the abovementioned get-together as a "feast of reason and flow of soul."

It is lonely at the top, and the head where lies the crown reigns heavy forsooth, but such is the cross that good wit must bear. The heads of entire communities must be indiscriminately cleaved from shoulders and spears must bring forth the water of endless sides, and the first in line are those who are full of it: The Artists.

There are also, however, populations whom Wodehouse held in slightly higher regard.

As mirth has now been proscribed across the United States and Laughter recently legislated punishable by firing squad, Wodehouse might have thought today's awoken zeitgeist a trifle tired and unmatey. During the early twentieth century, though,

Wodehouse had a fondness for the Yanks that makes one's chest swell with patriotic pride and one's heart long for the brass brand.

Wodehouse was born in Surrey, England, in 1881, and, in 1904—after a childhood there, an education in the South London suburbs at Dulwich College, and then two years under his father's tutelage as the laughingstock of the Hong Kong Bank—at the age of 23, he made his first trip to New York City and subsequently achieved nirvana. "Being there was like being in heaven without going through all the bother and expense of dying," he wrote. Therefrom, Wodehouse set out to write the missing mythology required of the New World, thereby creating his own language, which, as mentioned, is a necessity for anyone wanting to do wit right.

Wodehouse is credited as creating a truly novel mixture of U.S. and U.K. English. The Oxford English Dictionary credits Wodehouse in over 1,500 entries, 150 of which he is listed as the first known source for the word. An admirer of classical American cliches like *cracker jack* and *that's the way the cookie crumbles,* Wodehouse strived to make contributions to the American lexicon by way of coining now familiar terms such as *cuppa, loony-bin,* and *zippiness.* What made Wodehouse unique, however, was balancing Americanisms, such as *gentlemen's agreement, hotsy-totsy, dude, zing, fifty-fifty, ritzy, hooched, sweetie-pie,* and *bone-head* with unmistakable turn-of-the-century British working-class slang, such as *give me the pip* (irritate), *restore the tissues,* (drink), *off his onion* (unbalanced), and the Drones Club members' famed *What ho!* (hey!).

Yet, this mixture of U.S. and U.K. English would be for naught, were there not the appropriate U.S. and U.K. caricatures to put a talking melon atop the whole thing. With the creation throughout his works of over two thousand characters—twice that of Shakespeare's output—Wodehouse was no slouch in the character development department.

Indeed, Wodehouse employed these caricatures to write a kind of fantasy for Americans and British alike. For his American readers, he depicted the things for which we know Wodehouse best: the prelapsarian jolliness, the Edwardian romances, and the Old World-England that was more England than England has ever been. A universe of castles nestled within lush gardens; a sunny London full of young spiffs in spats and damsels cloaked in tweed, distress, and a fetching turn of phrase. Personal gentlemen's gentlemen were saying it well and doing it better. Cherrywood bedecked libraries, smokey private clubs, and gardening jihadists are standard. Portrayals of Bright Young Things, foolish fops, and boozed up gentlemen of leisure. All of it Americans take as gospel.

On the other side of the pond, British eyes were smiling at America's reputation for being somewhat prone to violence and crime. Consider Freddie Widgeon's destiny in "Fate," a short story from the 1936 collection *Young Men in Spats.* Freddie is in New York and on Cloud 9, having just affianced to the woman of his dreams. Despite his euphoria, he makes the observation that the appearance of those in New York seem as if, "everybody in the place were cutting up their wives and hiding them in sacks in the Jersey marshes or else putting detectives on them to secure the necessary evidence." Freddie also had some trouble taking in breakfast whilst reading a local newspaper, which featured "a photograph of Mae Elle McGinnis, taken when she was not looking her best because Mr McGinnis had just settled some domestic dispute with the meat-axe."

Soon thereafter, Freddie encounters a young woman struggling with a large suitcase that, due to its unusual weight, he states "appeared to be packed with sheet-iron or something." As a man who is soon to marry may help only unattractive young women not endowed with that special something, Freddie confirms this fact, braves the warm day, and assists the lady. After "having deposited female and suitcase at their destination," Freddie is offered a glass a water, a chair, and an interesting scene. Attempting to catch the suspectedly unfaithful Mrs. Silvers from apartment 4A getting familiar with a local gent, a group of bumbling American detectives bursts through the front door:

"'Ah!" said Bloke A, in a satisfied sort of voice...

"Seems to me," said the Bloke, addressing his associate Blokes, "this case is open and shut."

The other two nodded.

"That's right," said one.

"Open and shut," said the other.

"Yes," said the Bloke, summing up. That's about what it is. Open *and* shut."'

And, after one Bloke's announcing somewhat obviously that they found "Mrs Silvers alone in her apartment with this pie-faced cluck," the team was informed that they had bum-rushed one Miss Jennings of apartment 4B.

At the end of the story, Freddie Widgeon arrives back at that same apartment building to bring the woman whom he had helped back to his suspicious fiancée, so that his fiancée could see that this woman was, as Freddie notes, "a gargoyle." When upon this mission, he is asked by an exceedingly attractive neighbor to help her with opening a stuck window in her apartment. Out of chivalry, he acquiesces. Then, the "door flew open, and a number of large objects crashed in. Without any warning the air had suddenly become full of bowler hats."

The Boys are back:

"We're in boys," he said.

The two subsidiary blokes nodded briefly. One of them said: "sure we're in." The other said: "Hot dog!"

"...what's he doing here?"

"Opening the window."

"It's shut."

"I know it's shut."

"Open *and* shut," said the bloke. "Like the case. Eh, boys?"

"Ah!" Said one of the boys.

"Uh-huh," said the other.

Such scenes of distinctly American absurdity are no rarity in the works of Wodehouse: The once-betrothed American jewel thieves, Liz and Eddie, who fall in love again with each other years later in *Leave it to Smith*; broad-shouldered Jimmy Crocker, an American who, in *Piccadilly Jim,* gains the friendship of England's Lord Percy Whipple after whooping Whipple in a five-star restaurant; and, Bertie Wooster's very first adventure in the U.S. in "Extricating Young Gussie," the second short story in the collection *The Man with Two Left Feet,* during which Wooster overhears Gussie speaking with a gruff, hustling Broadway manager about acting in Vaudeville for peanuts on the dollar.

Wodehouse could not have created jokes about Americans if he did not feel comfortable in his new home. It is a measure of affection for his adopted country that he felt the need to recreate it in his fiction just as he had for his native country. And, in many ways, Wodehouse, a lad from Surrey, England, is one of the most American writers of the 20th century

During a 1923 stay in London, Wodehouse wrote, "all I want to do is to get back and hear the American language again." After decades of a trans-Atlantic relationship with the United States of America, which included stints of writing for Hollywood and Broadway, Wodehouse became an American citizen in 1955. In *America, I Like You,* published in 1956 and later titled *Over Seventy,* Wodehouse promised to tell, 'just the simple story of my love affair with the United States of America.'"

On February 14th, 1975, the Sublunary's lease on Sir Pelham Grenville Wodehouse was up, the Empyrean wanted its pound of flesh, and we have been paying dearly for it ever since.

Yet, just one month before this grave loss, Wodehouse was knighted in England as an Englishman. And, shortly after Valentine's Day, the writer who brought so much joy to so many readers, one of warmest-hearted authors ever to have existed, was buried in Long Island, New York—an American.

So, who else, then, might be a better representative for the introduction of writing in a culture's code?

For those interested in bunging down a droll line or two, there is a concept in good fiction writing that is invaluable. *The Reference Code,* also referred to as *The Cultural Code,* is way of writing by which a writer confidently appeals to a universal or consensual truth, or a body of shared cultural or scientific knowledge. Or, more succinctly, a way of writing that assumes that, by using this medium, the writer may jot down something subtle, and the reader will get it without the writer adding, "you know?" All of wit relies on this, as drawing attention to one's witticisms is the very death knell of them.

Instances of Cultural Code might include allusions or references to a culture's canon of literature, history, contemporary events, religious beliefs, moral values, or standards of decorum. One might need a smidgen of religious education to fully appreciate this zinger from Wodehouse's 1924 short story collection, *Ukridge*: "Take him for all in all, Mr. Nickerson looked like one of the less amiable prophets of the Old Testament about to interview the captive monarch of the Amalekites."

This image is very specific. And specific things have a chance of being accurate. And, as it is so rare, accuracy is an amusing thing to witness. We get something of a nervous laugh from the blunt facts. In other cases, it is a smirk of relief. Writing coded in the cypher of a culture should tell the truth, the whole truth, and nothing but the truth. But it is best that the truth be not too true. Consider the following shipments of wisdom on the sexes:

On Men:

> *...in the reverent voice in which men of business traditions speak of large sums.*
>
> *-Leave it to Psmith*

> *...in the early days of the honeymoon, when men are apt to do foolish things.*
>
> *-Leave it to Psmith*

And a man who is engaged to be married and who, already, is not too popular with the bride-to-be, shrinks—automatically, as it were—from blue-eyed, golden-haired females in pink negligees picked out with ultramarine love-birds.

-"Fate"

On Women:

She was the type of woman whom small, diffident men seem to marry instinctively, as unable to help themselves as cockleshell boats sucked into a maelstrom.

-Piccadilly Jim

A close observer would have marked a deepening of the look of pain on Mr Crocker's face. Women say this sort of thing [about sports] carelessly, with no wish to wound; but that makes it none the less heard to bear.

-Piccadilly Jim

Psmith embarked on his solitary meal, wondering sorrowfully at the perverseness which made girls work when there was no one to watch them.

-Leave it to Psmith

And the best code of all are the simple, daily occurrences that everyone can witness, experience, and make note of. Take, for example, Bertie Wooster's keen observation from *Code of the Woosters* about certain establishments of commerce:

> *...and, like all antique shops except the swanky ones in the Bond Street neighbourhood, dingy outside and dark and smelly within. I don't know why it is, but the proprietors of these establishments always seem to be cooking some sort of stew in the back room.*

Now, this bowls us smoothly into a slightly more general concept that I innovatively call *Creative Ways of Saying Simple Things*. Simple things are all around us, and, if you are simple, you will find them mundane. The good Wit, however, can make the instructions on the back of a tennis ball can into something of a good time. The idea here is to describe something simple without doing so directly. As instructors of foreign languages will tell you as you fumble your way through new vocabulary, if you are at a loss for the word, then you should try to describe *around* the idea. In fact, thinking of it in the sense of direction can be supremely helpful. The very copestone of *Leave it to Psmith*'s literary triumphs is often the most Psilent. Consider, then, Wodehouse's sense of direction when the meddling Baxter slips on a golf ball and falls down the stairs:

> *One uses the verb "'descend'" advisedly, for what is required is some word suggesting instantaneous activity. About Baxter's progress from the second floor to the first there was nothing halting or hesitating. He, so to speak, did it now. Planting his foot firmly on a golf-ball which the Hon. Freddie Threepwood, who had been practising putting in the corridor before retiring to bed, had left in his casual fashion just where the steps began, he took the entire staircase in one majestic, volplaning sweep. There were eleven stairs in all*

separating his landing from the landing below, and the only ones he hit were the third and tenth. He came to rest with a squattering thud on the lower landing, and for a moment or two the fever of the chase left him.

Instead of using cliche phrasing and tired images to convey that you are poor but not yet starving, attempt ones of your own assembly: "...you can't call me really one of the submerged tenth." Instead of stating the obvious by saying that working at a fish factory sucks and that you don't want to waste your life there, you might decide upon a creative Cultural-Code allusion to Medieval literature: "I like to be surrounded by joy and life, and I know nothing more joyless and deader than a dead fish. Multiply that dead fish by a million, and you have an environment which only Dante could contemplate with equanimity." Or, instead of stating unromantically that the angel with whom you're currently enjoying the sanctification of proximity is beautiful, you might actually show a little heart in the affair, describing the surrounding thoroughfare as if it were that very woman:

> *What strikes the visitor to London most forcibly, as he enters the heart of that city's fashionable shopping district, is the almost entire absence of ostentation in the shop-windows, the studied avoidance of garish display. About the front of the premises of Messrs. Thorpe & Briscoe, for instance, who sell coal in Dover Street, there is as a rule nothing whatever to attract fascinated attention. You might give the place a glance as you passed, but you would certainly not pause and stand staring at it as at the Sistine Chapel or the Taj Mahal. Yet at ten-thirty on the morning after Eve Halliday had*

> *taken tea with her friend Phyllis Jackson in West Kensington, Psmith, lounging gracefully in the smoking-room window of the Drones Club, which is immediately opposite the Thorpe & Briscoe establishment, had been gazing at it fixedly for a full five minutes. One would have said that the spectacle enthralled him. He seemed unable to take his eyes off it... it was his considered opinion that she improved the Thorpe & Briscoe frontage by about ninety-five per cent.*

What if one were able to string all of those creative ways of saying things together into a cohesive, self-contained creation driven by dramatic irony? There is meaning in every stroke, and it is all interconnected, and, if you blink, then you run the risk of missing it. If a story moves less like a contention with after-dinner bloat and more like a nimble creature flitting across the open plain, then it is likely plotted well.

There are a goodish many reasons why one might write a plot that plods—saunters in its pilgrimage over antique wooden bridges, stops to contemplate a riverside cowslip—but to incite action is not one of them. Wodehouse, amongst his many talents, is renowned for his successful snappiness of story and preeminent command of plot.

The pithiest approach to introducing a character whilst retaining one's dignity is through *gestures*, quiet things that a character might do or say that tell everything one needs to know about a character, without sending the reader away traumatized by exposition. *Ukridge* provides no such shortage of gestures:

"Laddie," said Stanley Featherstone Ukridge, that much enduring man, helping himself to my tobacco and slipping the pouch absently into his pocket, "listen to me, you son of Belial."

"What?"

"Do you want to make an enormous fortune?"

"I do."

"Then write my biography. Bung it down on paper, and we'll split the proceeds.

The book has had a lifespan of six sentences, and we have already smirked our way into knowing the man somewhat well.

"...we should clean up at least fifty thousand pounds apiece."

"As much as that?"

"Fully that. And listen, laddie, I'll tell you what. You're a good chap and we've been pals for years, so I'll let you have my share of the English serial rights for a hundred pounds down."

"What makes you think I've got a hundred pounds?"

"Well, then, I'll make it my share of the English and American serial rights for fifty."

"Your collar's come off its stud."

"How about my complete share of the whole dashed outfit for twenty-five?"

"Not for me, thanks."

"Then I'll tell you what, old horse," said Ukridge, inspired. "Just lend me half a crown to be going on with."

Give it half a page, and we feel as if we have been firm friends forever.

Wodehouse has herein accomplished in a moment what many writers cannot in a Russian triple-stacker. Gestures perform quick work. Here, there have already been nicknames, an attempt to nonchalantly swipe Corky's tobacco, a reference to Corky as the son of Belial, and the overview of a lofty business deal, which starts at a cool fifty thousand a piece. And, after Corky shows the proper interest in such a proposition by mentioning that Ukridge's collar has come off his stud, the deal is sealed with another sobriquet of "old horse," and the modest request to borrow a half crown before heading off. And there you have Stanley Featherstone Ukridge.

One will also notice that the story started with dialogue. After Wodehouse was asked if he had any tips for bright-eyed striplings endeavoring a hungry existence in the humor profession, he suggested that one should rush to the dialogue. Dialogue moves, by necessity, more quickly than narrative, as it provides the sense of immediacy.

A trilogy exists within this collection, the three titles of which are "The Debut of Battling Billson," The Return of Battling Billson," and "The Exit of Battling Billson," each of them absolute howlers. The basic idea is that a complete beast of a man who was put on this Earth to break bones ruins his certainty of pugilist stardom through his ludicrous idiosyncrasies. In *Debut,* Battling Billson is wounded to the knee by his soft spot for women. In *The Return,* he is bested by his own lack of intellect. In *The Exit,* he has adopted a peculiar set puritanical attitudes that express the general notion that the only thing more sinful than drinking is fighting. And there is no better place to start something, Wodehouse might say, than at the end.

"The Exit of Battling Billson" is a typically agile Wodehousian story with six major scene-location changes. We begin our jaunt at The Theatre Royal, Llunindnno, "that repellent town." It is here where our narrator, Corky, espies a "a large man...(whose) air was that of one who has recently passed through some trying experience." This is none other than the notorious Ukridge, and it is he who had just experienced the mild ignominy of being forcibly removed from the theatre abovementioned. After Corky denies Ukridge's request that he "bung a brick through the window," the story, only one-page-old, wastes no time in crawling us to a different public-house, in which a conversation is had, the story quickly develops, and the prospect of movement again looms large.

Said conversation involves such familiar tones as Ukridge's managing of Wilberforce Billson (Battling Billson), and how Ukridge "couldn't be more in the velvet if they gave him a sack and a shovel and let (him) loose in the Mint." After a moment's repartee about this less than likely aspect of fortune, Wodehouse shows no fear in beginning the next paragraph with Corky's reporting: "I was in a curiously uplifted mood on the following morning as I set out to pay my respects to Mr. Billson." Thus, in the minute span of three pages, we have already seen one day and been to three locations, presently culminating at another public house, where Mr Billson is "'spillin' (patrons') beers'" because "'Beer, he proceeded, with cold austerity, "'ain't right. Sinful, that's what beer is.'" Upon this sound conception, Wodehouse, without a description of walking from one place to another, frog-marches us to the next location: "I stood up on the steps of Number Seven Caerlon Street," Ukridge's place.

At Ukridge's digs, he and Corky discuss the unfortunate circumstance of Battling Billson's new puritanism, from which they suffer to learn that Billson, in addition to the consumption of adult beverages, now believes that "'fighting's sinful.'" With great dispatch, we are then teleported to Oddfellow's Hall, where Ukridge is looking as if he were next in line at the gallows and lacing the gloves on himself.

A comparatively long scene ensues, depicting Ukridge's surprising boxing aptitude. Yet, as the boxing match is viewed from more than a few angles, the scene feels something very much like movement or location change itself, each viewpoint containing new happenings. Alas, Ukridge's skills prove too little. But suddenly Battling Billson appears and, with a sudden and violent relapse into the throes of prizefighting, jumps into the ring and gives Ukridge's former competitor better sport.

This highly entertaining fiasco just barely over, "a hush fell" over the audience, and, with swiftness unmatched, we awaken at Ukridge's flat: The little sitting-room of Number Seven Caerleon Street was very quiet and gave the impression of being dark." The story completes itself, as all Wodehouse creations do, on-time—and wrapped up in an interconnected, ironic, full-circle ending.

Must every story thrive off a razor-sharp plot such as Wodehouse's? Yes—if one wants the feeling of movement and action, of sprinting alongside a story, just trying to keep up, as it were. The braver amongst of us might ask: but when do we transition scenes? Wodehouse would argue the answer to be right now.

Reasons to linger there are none; a sentence is all it takes to traipse villages, countries, ideas. This blitzkrieg of style is, at first, a challenge in plot. To be pithy enough to complete such a feat is, indeed, also a challenge in prose. More still, however, it is a challenge in wit. But above all else, Wodehouse is known for this: wildly creative, truly unprecedented imagery.

How does one introduce a literary feat of such electricity as the Wodehousian image? Novelist Tom Sharpe was getting the fork pretty close to the socket in *Plum*, a BBC documentary on Wodehouse, when he said that "you can never write a simile in a comic novel without being aware that it's been done better...I mean, Wodehouse more or less killed them."

Aside from an otherworldly writing routine and an exceedingly powerful imagination, Wodehouse had a masterful command of what has been defined as The Four Master Tropes. These Master Tropes have been deemed as playing the central role in the organization of entire systems of thought and therefore much of the literary sense. They are *metaphor, metonymy, synecdoche, and irony*. And, the long and short of the matter is that these tropes divide language, and therefore its product, imagery, into two corresponding parts: what is literally said and what is meant. For the purposes of imagery, we shall endeavor upon three of these four.

Let us start with the two that you do not know. What are metonymy and synecdoche? Simply, synecdoche a construction in which the writer creates an image that substitutes a part for a whole or whole for a part. This can be understood through common cliches, such as when we call a smart person a "brain," or a substitute on the football field "fresh legs." For metonymy, perhaps it is best to refer to Wodehouse.

In *Young Men in Spats*, Wodehouse begins each story as a retrospective yarn. The book begins with "It was the hour of the morning snifter, and a little group of Eggs and Beans and Crumpets had assembled in the smoking room of the Drones Club to do a bit of inhaling." Whereupon a "glassy-eyed silence...was broken by one of the Crumpets...then a Bean spoke..." then, an "Egg wistfully" sighed. In his short story "The Smile that Wins," from the collection *Mulliner Nights,* Wodehouse employs the same tactic, referring to the patrons "in the bar-parlor of the Angler's Rest" this time not as each element of the full English Breakfast, rather as the adult beverage of his choice. The conversation plays out with this general sentiment: "...said a Pint of Stout, vehemently...insisted a Whisky Sour...demanded a Mild and Bitter."

This is metonymy: a kind of substitution of the name of an attribute or an adjunct for the name of the thing meant. Needless to say, Eggs, Beans, and Crumpets do not allude only to a full English breakfast, the Pint of Stout, Whisky Sour, and Mild and Bitter not only to poison picked; the discrete elements of the ample breakfast and sundry beverages are the literal image, but the implied association is the appearance of someone, or "type" of person, who might likely enjoy that element of breakfast or that breed of tipple, and, in this way, embody what the each element of food or drink might represent—and perhaps even look like it—and that's dashed close to *anthropomorphism.*

Wodehouse's use of anthropomorphism, more commonly called personification, whenever describing an event to which he endeavored to bring great weight, was frequent. The husband after being frustrated by a controlling wife: "...a deep masculine silence fell." A perfectly lazy, midsummer's dream of an afternoon on the estate: "Blandings Castle dozed in the midsummer heat..." and, as a magnanimous king, "Silence reigned." Then, at night, "the smooth terrace slept under the stars," during which the burglary of Lady Constance's pearl necklace was taking place. Having hid the necklace in a flowerpot to be later retrieved in safety, Eve, the heroine of this story, now looks upon a flowerpot bereft of that same necklace, and "the flower-pot seemed the leer up at her in mockery."

At the risk of insulting the reader, I shall now note that similes are a sub-species of metaphor. Similes make implicit comparisons by designating the language of something to something else and use words *like, as if,* and *as though*; and one may achieve the same effect through *submerged similes,* which omit these words through originally fashioned comparative language. And the complete substitution of a word, image, or idea for another, based on an implied resemblance or analogy, is a metaphor.

Metaphors can help one see the unseeable, speak with the unknowable, and make sense of pure shadow. Unlike its cousin, the pun, metaphor is neither an immediate plea to reason nor a result of calculation; metaphor takes counsel from the eternal archetypes, summoning the intuition to experience a genuine likeness as if by intravenous. These express comparisons aid one to see everything as a reminder of something else and how the particular characterizes the universal. Indeed, like dreams, metaphors leave impressions of truths that awake the unconscious in a subtly profound way. And, through the employment of surprising juxtapositions of hitherto seemingly unrelated things, the metaphor and the joke have always been firm psychological friends.

As a fact, each and every time one encounters any of Wodehouse's hundreds of catalysts for comparison, which occur on every page, one witnesses an image blowing out the other side that tests the limits of one's VO2 Max. One could analyze the Wodehousian Image to death, but this method of analysis on the humorous image, though aboveboard enough, often lobs something of a wet sock into the proceedings. Too much theory to the imagination is like putting one's lips to the garden hose on a hot day and never taking them off. It kills what was a good thing. Indeed, what is needed is a church of examples, and I, for one, believe it to be better form to take them in and grease up the hassock for genuflection.

Images

Piccadilly Jim: "Mr Pett, on his side, receiving her cold glance squarely between the eyes, felt as if he were being disemboweled by a clumsy amateur."

"Fate": "...said Mavis, in a voice which would have left an Eskimo slapping his ribs and calling for the steam-heat..."

Ukridge: "He resembled a minor prophet who has been hit behind the ear with a stuffed eel-skin."

Ukridge: To hear this dignitary addressed—and in a shout at that—as "old horse" affected me with much the same sense of imminent chaos as would afflict a devout young curate if he saw his bishop slapped on the back.

"Bill The Bloodhound": If you would have asked him (sic) he would have said that he was a Scotch business man. As a matter of fact, he looked far more like a motor-car coming through a haystack.

"Bill The Bloodhound": That is to say, he felt like a cat which has strayed into a strange, hostile back-yard.

Leave It to Psmith: "drooping like a wet sock, as was his habit when he had nothing to prop his spine against..."

Joy in the Morning: "She came leaping towards me, like Lady Macbeth coming to get first-hand news from the guest room."

The Luck of the Bodkins: "Reggie looked like a member of the Black Hand trying to plot assassinations while hampered by a painful gumboil."

Jeeves in the Offing: "When she spoke, it was with the mildness of a cushat dove addressing another cushat dove from whom it was hoping to borrow money.

"The Man Who Disliked Cats": He was a Frenchman, a melancholy-looking man. He had the appearance of one who has searched for the leak in life's gas-pipe with a lighted candle; of one whom the clenched fist of Fate has smitten beneath the temperamental third waistcoat-button.

Spring Fever: His reputation is that of a man who, if there are beans to be spilled, will spill them with a firm and steady hand.

"The Editor Regrets": Any male turtle dove will tell you that, if the conditions are right, the female turtle dove can spit on her hands and throw her weight about like Donald Duck.

"The Spot of Art": The voice of Love seemed to call me, but it was a wrong number.

Big Money: "He groaned slightly and winced like Prometheus watching his vulture dropping in for lunch."

Mike and Psmith: "Some minds are like soup in a poor restaurant—better left unstirred."

Very Good, Jeeves: "Unseen in the background, Fate was quietly slipping lead into the boxing-glove."

"Jeeves and the Impending Doom": The Right Hon. was a tubby little chap who looked as if he had been poured into his clothes and had forgotten to say 'When!'

The Code of the Woosters: It is no use telling me that there are bad aunts and good aunts. At the core, they are all alike. Sooner or later, out pops the cloven hoof.

The Inimitable Jeeves: I turned to Aunt Agatha, whose demeanour was now rather like that of one who, picking daisies on the railway, has just caught the down express in the small of the back.

"The Crime wave at Blandings": When two men stand face to face, one of whom has recently shot the other with an airgun, and the second of whom has just discovered who did it, it is rarely that conversation flows briskly from the start.

Right Ho, Jeeves: She unshipped a sigh thar sounded like the wind going out of a rubber duck

Joy in the Morning: A wooden expression had crept into his features, and his eyes had taken on a look of cautious reserve which you see in those of parrots, when offered half a banana by a stranger of whose bona fides they are not convinced.

The Man Upstairs & Other Stories: "He had the look of one who had drunk the cup of life and found a dead beetle at the bottom."

Piccadilly Jim: "There were moments when he seemed on the verge of settling the matter, and then some invisible person would meanly insert a red-hot corkscrew in the stop of his head and begin to twist it, and this would interfere with calm thought."

Wodehouse's mastery of the English language subjects his readers—under the guise of laughter—to ancient mythology, the works of Shakespeare, and seminal historical events. Without any of the acrid taste of pretentiousness that oft coincides these authorial endeavors, he contributes his few words to The Great Conversation. Through sharp linguistical jabs, he leaves the last laugh up to the keen observer, leaving behind a barrage of quips, cracks, and badinage that exhaust superlatives to their gut-wrenching end and swathes them all up in a winsome getup of imagery that, to this day, remains unmatched.

Jerome K. Jerome

PERFECTLY RELIABLE NONSENSE

If one's voice found its natural tenor at what might be constituted as a disputatious row, then we would cease to believe that one were permanently angry, rather that one were simply irritating. If one's eyes resembled the First Flood at the sight of every minor misdeed the world puts forth, then we would in time decipher this candidate not to embody Empathy itself, rather Shallowness. Similarly, if it were one's predilection to encode all of one's statements with hidden meanings, then we would likewise soon understand this prevaricator as not infinitely interesting, rather as a potential purveyor of perpetually falsified information.

And it is this healthy suspicion of the extreme that may serve as the translation to why most contrivances of humor today are so outrageously unfunny: there lacks a baseline, irreverence palls as the new orthodoxy, and the signaling that one was "just kidding" makes the whole thing into a total joke. For a fix, seek no further than a therapeutically fetching dose of nineteenth-century irony.

Jerome K. Jerome's 1889 novel *Three Men in a Boat* is a marvel of decorous interpretations of the indecorous, deadpan observances of the grotesque, and—with the good conscience not to laugh at itself—tasteful overstatement of the mundane; it is a novel I should wager as a remedy for the recent comedic unpleasantness.

The first of two things paramount in aiding Jerome's writing so seminal a work of wit is his perfect balance of euphemism, overstatement, and understatement. The equilibrium of these powerful forces greatly enhances three of the most important elements of humor: tension, misdirection, and unpredictability. If things were, as they are now, one giant, ostentatious break of decorum, then all wit ceases to exist, and one is merely in observance of a kind of anarchy, a form of government entirely without nuance; therefore, let us investigate how we may instead use balanced diplomacy to our advantage.

By those much wiser than we, euphemism has been exposed over the last hundred years or so as "being fake" and "not keeping it real." The sagacious horde responsible for this social enlightenment reminds us that not all of us have been blessed with significant enough neurodiversity to aid our knowing the "Real" to be best represented by way of noisome grunts and bescumbered bludgeonings. However, we press onward in our ignorance, for we know euphemisms to be the direct path to a good laugh, and that is, after all, what we Cro-Magnons desire most.

Euphemisms are our baseline—a place of secure inoffensiveness—and come ready-made for humor, as their very existence depends on irony. Consider J., the narrator and main character of *Three Men in a Boat,* and his delineation of his many maladies to a local doctor, allegedly an "old chum" of J.'s. After listening to J.'s admonition that "Life is brief, and you might pass away before I had finished," as well as J.'s report that a medical dictionary has confirmed his possessing every illness and ailment of which science is aware, this old chum "opened [J.] and looked down [J.], and clutched hold of [his] wrist, and then [the doctor] hit [him] over the chest when [he] wasn't expecting it...and immediately afterwards butted [J.] with the side of his head." Whereupon, that same medical professional quietly sniffs out a hypochondriac and writes J. a prescription, which he "did not open."

When J. tenders this prescription to a local chemist, who "read it, and then handed it back," and "said he didn't keep it," J. asks if the man truly were a chemist, after which the chemist reveals his eagerness to assist J's store of general knowledge by admitting that "I am a chemist. If I was a co-operative stores and family hotel combined, I might be able to oblige you. Being only a chemist hampers me."

The prescription's contents:

1 lb beefsteak, with
1 pt bitter beer
Every six hours.
1 ten-mile walk every morning.
1 bed at 11 sharp every night.
And don't stuff up your head with
things you don't understand.

Was it required of the doctor diagnose our narrator as a malingerer, neurotic, or invalid? The answer seems to be in the negative. Temperate suggestions of beef, beer, and bedtime are heavy-handed enough. Neither was it altogether ungentlemanly of the pharmacist to answer in the oblique fashion that he did. Thus, through just a wee smidgen of propriety, delightful euphemisms occur, and lives are saved.

Altogether different from the recent modern phenomenon of comedy as a screaming-match of ill-conceived jokes concerning human genitalia, overstatement, in its classic form, is closer to a case of well-crafted emphasis that helps to express incongruity through the unpredictable. Overstatement can be easily achieved with something as simple as adding a contradictory adverb to a verb, thereby creating a variety of oxymoron, such as *remarkably unnoticeable*; *devastatingly plain*; *bewilderingly simple*; *distressingly soothing*.

For an overstatement with a bit more beef, we may consult J.'s story of his Uncle Podger's meeting some resistance whilst performing some minor home-improvements:

> *And then he would have another try, and, at the second blow, the nail would go clean through the plaster, and half the hammer after it, and Uncle Podger would be precipitated against the wall with force nearly sufficient to flatten his nose.*

Now that is an unbelievable hammer swing. And J.'s depiction soon thereafter of his Uncle Podger's doing a bit of DIY does double duty, for Uncle Podger's nose is not the only affected party:

> *Aunt Maria would mildly observe that, next time Uncle Podger was going to hammer a nail into a wall, she hoped he'd let her know in time, so that she could make*

arrangements to go and spend a week with her mother while it was being done.

It is common knowledge that the majority of work required of home-improvement projects is the repairing of marriages after near-divorce rows. True, not every man is a gifted carpenter, but even the tenderest of tenderfeet to handicraft would smirk at requiring more than a minute or so to drive a nail home. Therefore, calculating for deflation of ego, Maria's estimate of a week's time hits the nail on the head. Saint Maria more like.

Take into similarly deep consideration J.'s account of a local village's version of public transportation:

I called for the cheeses, and took them away in a cab. It was a ramshackle affair, dragged along by a knock-kneed, broken-winded somnambulist, which his owner, in a moment of enthusiasm, during conversation, referred to as a horse.

One indeed wonders how J. is privy to this horse's habits of slumber, as these are the more important questions to ask oneself whenever endeavoring upon a spot of creative embellishment.

But how is one's ability for Reason whilst under the influence of overstatement? Gain he or lose he what maketh Man divine? Well, I ask you, do statements such as these bring madmen to mind?

How good one feels when one is full – how satisfied with ourselves and with the world! People who have tried it, tell me that a clear conscience makes you very happy and contented; but a full stomach does the business quite as well, and is cheaper, and more easily obtained. One feels so forgiving and generous after a substantial and well-digested meal – so noble-minded, so kindly hearted.

Far be it from me to push the bounds of literary interpretation, but I should wager the key compound of this conceit to be "well-digested."

So, if euphemism be our baseline, and overstatement the way to jar readers with the stiff stuff, then understatement is our gentlemen's agreement, a subtle handshake that the writer enjoys with the reader without offending his sensibilities by asking if he "gets it," or by poking him repeatedly in the ribs to remind him of all the fun he is having. A well-written understatement is truly the king of humorous narrative-modes. The understatement is a sophisticated type of irony in which the speaker wants to be tactful and truthful at the same time, and true irony, much like the definition of true wit, is difficult to master, for it requires two meanings to be conveyed, one literal, the other intended. Furthermore, it is the tension between the two meanings that produces this ironic effect. *Three Men in a Boat* is a book whose main undercurrent is entirely that of understatement. In fact, the book is so drowned in it that to say that the novel employs understatement is itself an understatement of not inconsiderable magnitude; indeed, one laughs still more at the oft-held consideration that he might not be reading humor at all.

And the sophisticated narration of *Three Men in a Boat* is made possible by exactly this phenomenon: the mood and worldview of its narrator, who, despite floating gently down the Thames on a river-trip with his two best friends, is possessed by a strain of sardonicism that enters the darkly comic and invites readers to have a cackle at a very special species of schadenfreude.

To view our fellow man bedridden with sicknesses, illnesses, and maladies is absolutely no laughing matter—unless he has all of them. A neurotic fond of self-diagnosis is nowadays pitied in-person but is nevertheless a great source of humor once friends have gathered in the sitting room. And it is in the sitting room at the very beginning of the novel where J. admits that "[he] had just been reading a patent liver-pill circular, in which were detailed various synonyms by which a man could tell when his liver was out of order. [He] had them all." As J., George, and Harris are all martyrs to hypochondria and general seediness, we are then afforded the spectacle of a healthy competition throughout the book as regards who is really the sickest of the three and to what extent.

Harris, however, is special, according to J—especially dull, that is. And he is a friend. Yes, nothing gets the turbine of wit turning like a well-aimed shot at a long-time ally. Other than perhaps an enemy, what could better supply the hellish, jab-happy hands of wit than camaraderie? Is it not always a scene of comfort to watch two merry mates commit verbal assault upon each other in that way that makes the room shine with friendship? There is some of this shine indeed to J.'s suggesting that

> *You can never rouse Harris. There is no poetry about Harris – no wild yearning for the unattainable. Harris never 'weeps, he knows not why'. If Harris's eyes fill with tears, you can bet it is because Harris has been eating raw onions, or has put too much Worcester over his chop.*

Should not, then, the best beatdown be saved for the man's true best friend? J. finds further fisticuffs with his dog, Montmorency; and, in typical canine fashion, pooch gets the best of the interaction:

> *Montmorency's ambition in life is to get in the way and be sworn at. If he can squirm in anywhere where he is particularly not wanted, and be a perfect nuisance, and make people mad, and have things thrown at his head, then he feels his day has not been wasted.*
>
> *To get somebody to stumble over him, and curse him steadily for an hour, is his highest aim and object; and, when he has succeeded in accomplishing this, his conceit becomes quite unbearable.*

This slap-happiness, however, does not quite get the heart of the jocular suffering, but we are getting closer to it with the way that J. describes what it is like to eat whilst camping, reminding the reader that "[r]ainwater is the chief article of diet at supper."

The infamously impenetrable tin of pineapple scene is a classic for *Three Men in a Boat* enthusiasts, but I should venture that, slightly before the pineapple imbroglio, the moment that mentions the cold beef takes the cake. Of course, missing from this cold beef is mustard. It is here where we find the quiddity of the kind of misery with whom wit prefers company:

> *I don't care for mustard as a rule, and it is very seldom that I take it at all, but I would have given worlds for it then.*
>
> *I don't know how many worlds there may be in the universe, but anyone who had brought me a spoonful of*

> *mustard at that precise moment could have them all. I grow reckless like that when I want a thing and can't get it...*
>
> *...It cast a gloom over the boat, there being no mustard. We ate our beef in silence. Existence seemed hollow and uninteresting. We thought of the happy days of childhood, and sighed. We brightened up a bit, however, at the apple-tart, and, when George drew out a tin of pineapple from the bottom of the hamper, and rolled it into the middle of the boat; we felt that life was worth living after all.*

Thus, to shamelessly gormandize upon embellishment whilst blatantly semaphoring one's every half-baked machination is the witless way of humorless clowns. Do not be like these people. Do not be fooled by the masses who laugh at misery masquerading as a good time. Instead, seek a good time masquerading as what seems like misery. Seek the bad news turned good. Seek the grotesque turned commonplace. Seek the ludicrous turned monotonous. Seek the truth.

Forsooth, it is this forthright style of observation in conjunction with a resignation to the colorfully miserable that tempers one's wit much like a smith would improve the hardness and elasticity of a fine blade; or, as Jerome K. Jerome himself wrote in his Preface to the First Edition his work,

> *The chief beauty of this book lies not so much in its literary style, or in the extent and usefulness of the information it conveys, as in its simple truthfulness...Other works may excel this in depth of thought and knowledge of human nature: other books may rival it in originality and*

> *size; but, for hopeless and incurable veracity, nothing yet discovered can surpass it.*

The best way to tell the truth is by lying: It is cold in Death Valley; the right politician will solve your problems; your phone is not listening to you. Humans, for good reason, love falsehood. Germans, however, have always computed humans strange for this very purpose, and have therefrom attempted, on numerous separate instances, without much success, to inform humans of The Truth. This is all due to the fact that they do not teach irony or satire in German schools, as it is illogical to do so and often leads to a terminal condition called Laughter. This might sound scientific enough, but the Germans, it is true, have been misrepresented. Written in 1900, Jerome K. Jerome's *Three Men on the Bummel,* the accompaniment novel to *Three Men in a Boat,* through its earnest employment of the rhetorical form of *Adynaton,* commits a recognizable depiction of the Teuton that finally does the Fatherland some much-deserved national justice, detailing the German amidst his favorite subjects of Law and Order.

Adynaton is extreme hyperbole. It pushes the boundaries of exaggeration to the absurd, thereby telling far more than the mere truth; it supplies an armature of theory, value, and meaning to that straight, basic truth that otherwise would be without context, be without the slant. And, although Jerome claims that "[he] wishes this book to be a strict record of fact, unmarred by exaggeration…," by dedicating the entirety of his book to the art of resourceful lying, he seems to go against his word.

The beautiful disorder of nature is the only thing left untrammeled by Man's modern machines. Not so in Germany. Consider Jerome's unbiased reports as regards his observations whilst in the Land of Order: "In Germany one breathes in love of order with the air, in Germany the babies beat time with their rattles, and the German bird has come to prefer the box and regards with contempt the few uncivilized outcasts who continue to build their nests in trees and hedges." From here, consider further Jerome's observations of the German's recondite relation between the state of nature and his ability to rest: "Your German likes nature...He plants seven rose trees on the north side and seven on the south, and if they do not grow up all the same size and shape, it worries him so that he cannot sleep nights." A similar vein of rationality continues with the knowledge that the main character, J., bestows as regards how the German prefers his trail-hike: "He likes his walk through the wood—to the restaurant. But the pathway must not be too steep, it must have a brick gutter running down one side of it to drain it, and every twenty yards or so it must have its seat on which he can rest and mop his brow." And, on this buccaneering route to adventure, "There will be a seat every fifty yards, a police notice every hundred, and a restaurant every half-mile." Whereupon, if, whilst *auf dem Wandern,* the German encounters inclement weather, "unable to regulate...so unruly a thing as the solar system, he ignores it." Moreover, "If, in addition, he can find a police notice posted on a tree forbidding him to do something or other, that gives him an extra sense of comfort and security," as the only thing the German respects more than Order is Law.

As Jerome elucidates for the general readership, the German's a Lawful kind "...whose only ambition appears to be to pay his taxes, and do what he is told to do...He is willing, nay, anxious, to be controlled and regulated in all things." The apotheosis of law to the German is the policeman. And that is no exaggeration: "The policeman is to him a religion." This deification begins from the very first for the German, as "It is the hope of every well-meaning German boy and girl to please the police...(a) German child that has been patted on the head by a policeman is not fit to live with; its self-importance is unbearable." And, as the German *Junge* grows into a young man, it is implicitly understood that "The German citizen is a soldier, and the policeman is his officer. The policeman directs him where in the street to walk, and how fast to walk. At the end of each bridge stands a policeman to tell the German how to cross it." But, unlike other countries, wherein this draconian nightmare would incite chatter of individual liberty and murmurs of revolution, "in Germany you take no responsibility upon yourself whatever. Everything is done for you, and done well... It is the duty of the German policeman to look after you...and he takes good care of you...there is no denying this." Many nations possess meaningful mottos pithily illuminating that same nation's longstanding cultural history. Jerome informs us of Germany's: "'you get yourself born,' says the German government to the German citizen, 'we do the rest.'" According to Jerome's further dispassionate accounts on the matter, the German's dedication to Law is not merely confined to matters of life:

> *I do not know if it be so, but from what I have observed of the German character I should not be surprised to hear that when a man in Germany is condemned to death he is given a piece of rope, and told to go and hang himself...and I can see that German criminal taking that piece of rope*

> *home with him, reading up carefully the police instructions, and proceeding to carry them out in his own back kitchen.*

And, even after that law-abiding German carries out upon himself the ultimate sentence, Jerome suggests that the lawful deeds of *der deutschen Polizei* are never quite over:

> *The Germans are a good people...I am positive that the vast majority of them go to heaven... [that the] the soul of a single individual German has [however] the sufficient initiative to fly up by itself and knock on St. Peter's door, I cannot believe. My own opinion is that they are taken there in small companies, and passed in under the charge of a dead policeman.*

I, for one, take this last description as a joke. Firstly, to assert that the Germans are a good people seems, to me, a premise of pure opinion, and the conclusion of the German's entrance into heaven is just plain immeasurable. It would be impossible to know. But, even more of an affront to those *Übermenschen* is Jerome's notion that Germans wandering in the afterlife still do not possess the proper autonomy to inquire about their evening's accommodations. This is an extreme exaggeration, patently offensive, and—the notion that they would need a dead policeman to do so—positively absurd.

Mark Twain

RHETORICALLY ROUGHING IT

Mark Twain was not a genius. In fact, his biography is marred by the types of blemishes indicative of a first-rate fool: low education, low income, high unemployment, frequent vagrancy, recurrent profligate business ventures, et cetera—indeed, everything we monitor for today on our little credit-risk charts whenever we are deciding who gets to live or die. How is it, then, that we praise this penniless backwater yokel as The Grandfather of American Literature? Mark Twain is a master of the memorable line, a champion of leaving us in awe at a turn of phrase. He undoubtedly possesses the roguish slant required of a good writer of the Picaresque, but being a disreputable swashbuckler alone does not propel one to become one of the finest Wits literature has ever known. The disappointing secret is that Mark Twain practiced, a lot. More specifically, this past master of the quip diligently practiced the figures of rhetoric. Like all great writers before him, who make us contemporary hacks want to close up shop just by glancing at the page, Twain mercilessly enforced on himself the conscientious employment of what the Ancient Greeks had invented and developed for the sole purpose of persuasion and delight. Twain's bravura of Western Frontier hilarity, *Roughing It*, is a scintillating showcase of wit, and, by casting an interested glance at Twain's frequent use of the figures of rhetoric therein, one may ascertain that the ability to dazzle is not divinely endowed to the chosen few, but rather may be learnt by anyone, even foolhardy hicks.

Yet, despite its ability to be learnt by even the foolhardiest, the discipline of rhetorical devices is nevertheless an intriguing, complex, and rather sizable one, and I claim not to have the sacred alchemical text, which I had once supposed existed, that distills this discipline into a simple concoction of elementary algebraic formulas to plug in whenever the words aren't flowing and the going gets generally rough.

However, during my years of autodidactic ganders around the buffet of rhetoric, one thing has certainly become clear to me: people like patterns. The figures of rhetoric are patterns; therefore, people like the figures of rhetoric. They're not always aware that they like them, but they do, just as people are not always aware of patterns.

Twain cooked up a great many clever narrative and literary devices in *Roughing It*, as well as a smorgasbord of rhetorical schemes. There are some rhetorical schemes, however, that render one's writing as appearing especially intelligent, snappy, and quick—schemes that raise the brow of what is often called one's "turn-of-phrase." In truth, *Roughing It* is nothing other than an elite-level exercise in turn-of-phrase, hence, to chronicle every occurrence therein would be an impossibility. Therefore, I shall focus herein on a few instances of particularly pithy and playful forms of rhetoric that I believe would begin one's way on the path to a fine turn of phrase, starting with everyone's favorite: alliteration.

Alliteration is everyone's favorite rhetorical scheme for two reasons: it pleases the ear and makes the author seem craftier than he really is. Consider Twain's depiction of the aftermath of eleven Mormon wives demanding a valuable love-trinket from their husband: "Eleven promised breastpins purchased peace once more." In this case, in addition to having a lovely rhythm, the four ps were placed punctiliously. Alliteration should, however, be used with the utmost judiciousness, lest one begins to sound foolish. The previous example, although it works well, pushes the proper bounds of what is plainly possible. Whenever alliteration occurs in sequences of more than two, a ridiculous, even grating effect can begin to take effect. Whenever used with extreme care, however, it is a most mellifluous piece of rhetoric. Consider the pleasant hum of Twain's honey-sweet hearkenings back to a fine, sunny morning in the West with a Mormon wagon convoy:

> *Toward dawn we got under way again, and presently as we sat with raised curtains enjoying our early-morning smoke and contemplating the first splendor of the rising sun as it swept down the long array of mountain peaks, flushing and gilding crag after crag and summit after summit, as if the invisible Creator reviewed his gray veterans and they saluted with a smile, we hove in sight of South Pass City.*

One exhausts one's mental faculties at what this muddle of English would even be without the letter "s." At its best, alliteration audibly mimics the writerly action or idea one wants to convey: the soft sibilance of the flooded freshets. Hear the water?

Shall we move on? Rhetorical Questions are a surprisingly powerful form of rhetoric on account of not providing room for an answer. And we tend to like answers. Moreover, rhetorical questions often signal something important to which we should likely lend a cellphoneless ear. And what could be more important than contemplating the final thoughts of dead man? In one of the hundreds of *Roughing It*'s wildly spun yarns, Twain tells the tale of a fool climbing the "perilous peaks of Mont Blanc and the Matterhorn," who "comes darting down the long mountain-crags in a sitting posture" and generally encounters all prospects of pain imaginable during his joyride down. Shortly thereafter, Twain asks us to question the consequences of such recreation: "This is all very fine, but let us not be carried away by excitement, but ask calmly, how does this person feel about it in his cooler moments next day, with six or seven thousand feet of snow and stuff on top of him?"

Similarly, reflect upon Twain's usage of rhetorical questioning as he critiques Adam Smith's magnum opus, the Mormon Bible, and its depiction of certain past followers ascending to heaven: "and they were in number about two thousand and five hundred souls; and they did consist of men, women, and children." To which, Twain posits: "And what else would they be likely to consist of?" But how is one to answer a question like that?_

Due to its inherently eloquent absurdity, a particular favorite form amongst humorous Wits is the Transferred Epithet. The mental outcome of encountering a transferred epithet is usually a species of pleasant confusion. Essentially, the transferred epithet as an adjective that is applied to a noun to which one would rightfully believe the adjective should not be applied, but the psychological effect of the syntax leaves things nevertheless as intuitive as ever, and we understand immediately the meaning.

This is a rhetorical form, it must be said, for which not Mark Twain, but rather P.G. Wodehouse is most famous. With Wodehousean Earth-shatterers such as "an astonished piece of toast" and "...I sat in the bathtub, soaping a meditative foot...," it is not exactly hard to see why Plum takes the cake. But Twain was not exactly sawing logs during his shift either. Cogitate on Twain's eating of "a hasty breakfast." The last I checked, (but we do live in progressive times) morning meals have not the ability to move, let alone with the relative consistency to be judged by their speed. Of course, the line referred to Twain's character eating a breakfast hastily, but I am certain that Twain did not mean this book to be used as a soporific, and so he used a transferred epithet instead of boring his readers to sleep.

Evidence of humans' affection for symmetry is everywhere. We find it incredibly pleasing to look upon, and even use it to decide on both our landscaping and our lifelong mates. It is only logical, then, that we might find some private stimulation whenever it is found in print. Unfortunately, our senses are rather consistently assailed by many an unattractive sentence shaped like the following: We enjoy drinking, fighting, and some sex.

This rather warm-blooded statement includes a successful first-person plural pronoun as its subject, an intransitive verb describing their feelings on the matter, and two spirited gerunds pertaining to how these ruffians find pleasure. Then, just at the climax of the series, a break in symmetry renders what was at first an exciting sentence flaccid: instead of a third gerund to complete the trinity, a grotesque adjective is placed before a common noun, thus rendering it all a formless heap.

Isocolon is the shapely antidote to this heap. Isocolon is, simply put, a sentence devised of alike parts, with a construction grammatically alike or symmetrical in form and therefore structurally matching. And Twain had the abovementioned formless heap on his mind when he penned a trifle about a curiosity in American Frontier currency: "…if one wanted a cigar, it was a quarter; if he wanted a chalk pipe, it was a quarter…" Neat, dashing, and easy on the eyes.

But the figures of rhetoric need not be sold separately. The isocolon in the sentence above is clear, but what about the instances of Anaphora and Epistrophe? Anaphora is whenever one begins each clause, sentence, or paragraph with the same word(s); epistrophe is whenever one finishes each clause, sentence, or paragraph with the same word(s). But don't take my word(s) for it, instead stuff a second glance of that same line on the cigar and the pipe into ocular apertures and smoke hard on it.

Likewise, examples of Polyptoton, Anadiplosis, and innumerable other rhetorical delights parade on through this absolute fourth of July fireworks show of a book with a jingoistic pageantry unmatched. It is the sad, solemn truth, though, that there would be no Twain at all without hyperbole.

Certainly, there is not a better bold-faced liar on the planet than Samuel Langhorne Clemens—play me the fool again, Samuel, we seem to say. And what is hyperbole but fibbing in the right spirit? Consider Twain's enjoyable propaganda as regards the staggering width of the Humboldt River: "One of the pleasantest and most invigorating exercises one can contrive is to run and jump across the Humboldt River till he is overheated, and then drink it all dry." I have never been to, seen, or even know where the Humboldt River is, but my suspicions lead me in the direction that this activity be exaggerated.

And that's really the rub: Twain's rhetorical muscle is fully flexed whenever he is telling very, very tall tales. Whenever he uses an animal to fashion that falsehood, he is truly at full horsepower, just as he does when he describes how his stallion is frightened by a heated bull: "[it] seemed to literally prostrate my horse's reason... stand on his head for a quarter of a minute and shed tears." To evade this bull, our narrator hauls himself up a tree. On Twain's Frontier, however, the possible is the certain and the impossible is just a matter of time.

Imagine how "[he] watched the bull, now, with anxiety—anxiety which no one can conceive of who has not been in such a situation and felt that at any moment death might come... Sure enough, it was just as I had dreaded, he started in to climb the tree..." From here,

> *The bull started up, and got along well for about ten feet, then slipped and slid back. I breathed easier. He tried it again—got up a little higher—slipped again. But he came at it once more, and this time he was careful. He got gradually higher and higher, and my spirits went down more and more. Up he came—an inch at a time—with his eyes hot, and his tongue hanging out. Higher and higher—hitched his foot over the stump of a limb, and looked up, as much as to say, 'You are my meat, friend.'*

Another modest example contains a mildly gluttonous camel:

In Syria, once, at the head-waters of the Jordan, a camel took charge of my overcoat while the tents were being pitched, and examined it with a critical eye, all over, with as much interest as if he had an idea of getting one made like it; and then, after he was done figuring on it as an article of apparel, he began to contemplate it as an article of diet. He put his foot on it, and lifted one of the sleeves out with his teeth, and chewed and chewed at it, gradually taking it in, and all the while opening and closing his eyes in a kind of religious ecstasy, as if he had never tasted anything as good as an overcoat before, in his life. Then he smacked his lips once or twice, and reached after the other sleeve. Next he tried the velvet collar, and smiled a smile of such contentment that it was plain to see that he regarded that as the daintiest thing about an overcoat. The tails went next, along with some percussion caps and cough candy, and some fig-paste from Constantinople

And then my newspaper correspondence dropped out, and he took a chance in that—manuscript letters written for the home papers. But he was treading on dangerous ground, now. He began to come across solid wisdom in those documents that was rather weighty on his stomach; and occasionally he would take a joke that would shake him up till it loosened his teeth; it was getting to be perilous times with him, but he held his grip with good courage and hopefully, till at last he began to stumble on statements that not even a camel could swallow with impunity. He began to gag and gasp, and his eyes to stand out, and his forelegs to spread, and in about

> *a quarter of a minute he fell over as stiff as a carpenter's work-bench, and died a death of indescribable agony. I went and pulled the manuscript out of his mouth, and found that the sensitive creature had choked to death on one of the mildest and gentlest statements of fact that I ever laid before a trusting public.*

Mark Twain is the best American humorist and Wit to date and stands as a shining example of what one can do whenever one is not afraid of a bit of practice. The forms of rhetoric are proven formulas against the perfunctory and the prosaic. Slave not after the Romantic notion of untutored artistic afflatus. This is a swindle. The Romantics all had Classical educations before they decided school was for fools. School should never be over. Twain voraciously devoured the Classics, drank in the Oxford Unabridged Dictionary as much as any novel, and diligently practiced the figures of rhetoric. *Roughing It,* one of the most sophisticated and awe-inspiring works of American fiction, was written by a former steamboat pilot and self-proclaimed tramp with a fifth-grade education.

Evelyn Waugh

HOME ALONE: WAUGH, THE WANDERING WIT

The Home is a place of infinite comfort and belonging, an inviolable bower to one's identity. A Home may, but need not be, a physical place; its entreaties can be procured through such means as adherences to hierarchies of being, objective moralities, powers of the Divine, a profound mystification with Nature, and a purposeful relation towards existence. But Homes, though secure, are solemn, immobile creatures and therefore not conducive to the allusive wanderings of wit. Wit may never come home, for, if it did, it would cease to resemble wit at all, taking on instead the stoic visage of soporific sermon. Wit is secular; it allows positively zero room for worship. Unless, of course, you were a satirist. Should you be a devout Catholic satirist, then my definition doesn't hold up well at all: it's wholly water. The delightfully snappish satirist, Evelyn Waugh, indeed defies definition with his sui generis whip up of wildly waggish wit and religious obsession with The Home, an obsession ironically conveyed through a lifetime of biting satires riddled with homelessness.

Of satire, there are essentially three forms: Horatian, Juvenalian, and Menippean, invented by Horace, Juvenal, and Menippus, respectively. Each style has a different position towards critique. As I understand it, Horatian satire is akin to gently correcting the behavior of a cherished group of friends by kindly suggesting refinement through warm-hearted raillery. Juvenalian is reserved for whenever one is having a particularly bad day and interested in a full-frontal knuckle-up with the perceived object responsible for that day's downward trajectory, often people or institutions. And Menippean is something a bit more abstract, something like inviting those with distasteful ideas and mental attitudes into one's own home and speaking with them about those same ideas and mental attitudes that one finds to be ready for the trash can. Then, without attributing this garbage to them directly, choosing instead to soften things up a trifle by suggesting betterment through analogy, metaphor, or allegory. In this form, extraordinary settings and narrative abstraction are quite common.

Unlike other forms of humor that rely on generally unbiased observations of human behavior and its foibles, satire operates by placing its selected subject matter under a certain scorn, derision, or ridicule, with the hope that, by doing so, a shock of recognition will jolt through the reader that renders one repulsed by the hitherto uncontemplated vice or folly and in desire of dispossession at the personal or societal level. And a particularly successful satire will have convinced its reader that all will benefit from the banishment of the iniquity exposed and denounced therein.

And, if this reads as at all religious in temperament to you, you are neither imagining things nor gaslighting yourself, for satire requires a special something promised by the Divine: judgement.

Satire exists exactly because of its element of judgement, which, channeled through the satirist's belief system, originates in the satirist's idea of a more perfect world. The perceived negative elements of personality, philosophy, or society to be receiving the axe are juxtaposed against the satirist's ideal conceptions thereof, which are championed in a way that should assure the reader of the superiority of those ideals. But a rusty broadsword to the thorax, although diplomatic, won't quite do here. While satire is, without a doubt, an attack, its vanguard lead neither with lash out nor lambast—seldomly effective routes—rather with burlesque and humorous irony. A spoonful of sugar makes the satire go down roughshod, and its recuperative effects should eschew the taste of destruction as much as possible, in favor of a constructive relish.

Waugh's satires are no strangers to judgement. His work neglects to go as far as Dante, who placed those with whom he disagreed literally in hell, but Waugh's efforts at moral concealment are, nevertheless, sometimes a little thin. Conversely, Waugh's narrative style favors a lighter, understated approach, and his settings are always deeply metaphorical in nature, thereby creating clever, Menippean microcosms that animate Waugh's beliefs on sundry topics, greatest of which is his savage disdain for all things Modern. An easy place to start for a peep into the burlesque side of things might be with Waugh's 1932 collar-tugging classic *Black Mischief*.

The best satire thrives on intrepid comparisons, and *Black Mischief* does more than its fair share of the heavy lifting to achieve this necessity. Notorious for its colorful assault on the natives of the fictional African island of Azania—who display zero capacity for Reason, show even less impulse-control, foment incessant tribal warfare of a particularly violent kind, and enjoy heaping helpings of rampant cannibalism—the book sets the Azanians up as a fairly good starting place for the definition of pure barbarism. Yet, sadly, it is here where some of today's slightly more Cro-Magnon readers stop, scratch their bottoms, and don the loincloth of primitive literalism. Indeed, not only is Waugh an equal opportunity satirist, giving it to the Europeans—in fact, to all humans in the text—with both barrels, but it would be missing the joke by a Detroit mile, if one did not understand what Waugh were truly satirizing: Modernity.

Seth, the supreme leader of Azania, addresses himself in every letter as the "Chief of Chiefs," "Lord," and "Tyrant," but also as the marginally more sober "Bachelor of the Arts of Oxford University." After his brief period of study in England, there is nothing that Seth wants more than to modernize his homeland of Azania. However, despite his best efforts to highjack the modern European sentiment, his Azanian instincts prevent him from ever really understanding what Modernity is, much less how its tenets are to be properly implemented into society. He says that "My people are a worthless people. I give orders; there is none to obey me. I am like a great musician without an instrument...I must find a man of culture, a modern man...a representative of Progress and the New Age."

Basil Seal, the book's shiftless main character, was to be that man.

And although generally disliked in England and having just pinched his mother's emerald bracelet weeks before to pay for his ship ticket to Azania, "Basil stood to [Seth] as the personification of all that glittering, intangible Western culture to which he aspired." Shortly after Basil's arrival, Basil founds The Ministry of Modernization. From there, the One Year Plan to modernize this wasteland has begun.

The choice to use a religious word in the name of its secular institution aside, the Ministry of Modernization is off to an intelligent and robust start. It is described as "a circulatory building of concrete and corrugated iron, its outer wall enriched with posters from all parts of Europe and the United States advertising machinery, fashion, and foreign travel." Or, simply put, any ugly, modern city block. Inaugurated shortly thereafter are the State Lottery and the plans to knock down the Anglican Cathedral. Seth soon asks Basil, "How much are autogyros?...Tell me exactly, please, what is Surrealism?" Moreover, Seth shows high interest in "a German architectural magazine and had decided to have the new building constructed in steel and vita-glass," which sounds an awful lot like the aesthetic zenith reached by the contemporary office building. Thus, in no time at all, Azania "lost all evidence of national character." Here, it is an instance of very minor mental travail to envision this as also a description of our contemporary world.

But let us not forget the liturgy of the Modern life: bureaucracy. Seth's initial "decree was to promote the adoption of modern organization and habits of life throughout the Azanian Empire, which liberally interpreted, comprised the right of interference in most of the public and private affairs of the nation." Two shakes later and there were upon Basil's desk seas of "documents full of ponderous expressions of politeness and the minimum of trustworthy information...applications for concessions...inquiries from the tourist bureaux...applications for public appointments;

protests from missions and legations; estimates for building; [and] details of court etiquette and precedence..." Whereafter, Basil informs the local gazette owner that he "want(s) to buy (his) paper." And nothing communicates the Modern experience quite like biased media. The Society for the Prevention of Cruelty of Animals soon gets the classic Azanian twist, becoming the slightly less noble Cruelty to Animals Commission.

The most curious moment of burlesque, however, occurs in the Azanian population's interpretation of the effects of birth control. When Basil introduces the topic to Seth, Seth says, "I must have a lot of that. We must popularize by propaganda—educate people in sterility." This is realized through the following placarded advertisement and subsequent public interpretation:

> *It portrayed two contrasted scenes. On one side a native hut of hideous squalor, overrun with children of every age, suffering from every physical incapacity—crippled, deformed, blind, spotted and insane; the father prematurely aged with paternity squatted by an empty cook-pot; through the door could be seen his wife, withered and bowed with child-bearing, desperately hoeing at their inadequate crop. On the other side a bright parlour furnished with chairs and table; the mother, young and beautiful, sat at her ease eating a huge slice of raw meat; her husband smoked a long Arab hubble-bubble (still a caste mark of leisure throughout the land), while a single healthy child sat between them reading a newspaper. Inset between the two pictures was a detailed drawing of some up-to-date contraceptive apparatus and the words in Sakuyu:* WHICH HOME DO YOU CHOOSE?

> *Interest in the pictures was unbounded; all over the island woolly heads were nodding, black hands pointing, tongues clicking against filed teeth in unsyntactical dialects. Nowhere was there any doubt about the meaning of the beautiful new pictures.*
>
> *See: on right hand: there is rich man: smoke pipe like big chief: but his wife she no good; sit eating meat: and rich man no good: he only one son.*
>
> *See: on left hand: poor man: not much to eat: but his wife she very good, work hard in field: man he good too: eleven children: one very mad, very holy. And in the middle: Emperor's juju. Make you like that good man with eleven children.*

The public demonstration in support of birth control held soon thereafter, during which banners that included such hopeful snippets as "Women of Tomorrow Demand an Empty Cradle" and "Through Sterility to Culture," is met with spirited opposition and swiftly overthrown. And it is sometime around this mark when "on Basil the strain of modernity began to leave its traces."

And this is Waugh's real beef.

The very title of *Black Mischief* is a daring pun on the witchcraft performed upon the Western populace—indeed upon all of humanity—by Modernity's cunning hand. And Waugh's final judgement is that all of humanity is to blame. To participate in Modernity is to be as barbarous as a proper barbarian, for both walks of life call for a Godless world. The Modern Man, like the barbarian, knows no hierarchy of being, objective morality, connection to the Divine, mystification with Nature, nor purposeful relation towards existence. As Prudence, Basil's love interest who was later chopped up by natives and cooked in a stew to be unknowingly eaten by Basil, writes in her journal, *How out of tune with Nature is the spirit of man!*

It does not take a journey to a fictional island off the coast of Africa, however, to experience the wasteland at its worst. One can enjoy that privilege from the comfort of home. *A Handful of Dust* follows Tony Last: passable father, beyond-uxorious husband, and enthusiastic proprietor of Hetton Abbey, "formerly one of the notable houses of the county" turned Gothic laughingstock that is now "devoid of interest" to all but one. In contrast to *Black Mischief*, *A Handful of Dust* depicts, as Waugh affectionately described it, "the savages at home" and gives the satirical technique of burlesque the old garden rake to the nose in preference for an all-you-can-suffer irony-fest. Said fiesta is achieved through a fertile and ubiquitous theme of usurpation. Specifically, a usurpation of the Home through Modernity. In this way, the struggles of Tony Last are the struggles of England, and the struggles of England the struggles of all.

Since its inception in the Enlightenment era, Modernity has been defined by its retreat from the Divine, commitment to scientific objectivity, stark disconnection from Nature, estrangement from objective morality, and a loss of patriarchal connection. This departure from a wide variety of long-standing human traditions slowly skewed the consciousness of humanity away from any form of meaning—creating something of a slipped disc of the mind. And, by *A Handful of Dust*'s 1934, society is beyond reaching for the IcyHot.

Although Modernity purports itself to be the catalyst for some of the greatest achievements of European life, such as urban, cosmopolitan civilization, material prosperity, a methodologically secure, rationally grounded science, and the then radical notion of individual liberty, other alluring products, such as mass-scale alienation, disaffection, a fatuous culture of commercialized kitsch, and the overwhelming sense of a stultifying, boring, even pointless life were likewise readily available.

And it is this second bit about which a few souls held reservations. While many were, by the 19th Century, guzzling the grog of Modernity with unchecked jubilation, some were dipping teaspoons into the punchbowl and squinting skeptically. Forest-worshipping Romantics and Christian cultural conservatives alike rejected the modern way of life, suggesting Modernity a demeaning routinization of life, altogether a corruption, and a complete spiritual disaster. The whole cosmos of the modern economic order was now but an iron cage that produces specialists without spirit and sensualists without heart. Therefore, a life that quests after the pre-modern sentiment and values, both groups would deem, is a life on the winning team. Why, then, does Tony Last, family man, Gothic architecture fanatic, and unfailing churchgoer—the very antithesis to the modern human and everyone in the book—lose so hard?

The terrible fate that befalls Tony ensues because he is a complete spineless fake.

For starters, his practice of religion is purely formal; church is "jolly" and "most agreeable." During the services he is occasionally struck by a phrase of the liturgy, but for the most part he is preoccupied with plans for installing bathrooms and lavatories at Hetton. A Church service "followed its course...as Tony inhaled the agreeable, slightly musty atmosphere and performed the familiar motions of sitting, standing, and leaning forward, [and] his thoughts drifted from subject to subject, among the events of the past week and his plans for the future." Of course, one might think that this is just what we all do at church, so where is the big sin? And that is precisely Waugh's point.

Now let us take a look at the familial side of things. Brenda, Tony's wife—even immediately after the death of her only son by way of horse hoof to skull—is boastfully adulterous, unabashedly condescending, and pretends to be studying economics in order to keep an apartment in London to repeatedly exert herself upon John Beaver, local dud, joker, and mama's boy. During this time, she gallivants with the likes of Polly Cockpurse and Princess Jenny Abdul Akbar, the latter of whom Brenda attempts to pass off to her husband but whom Tony calls a "joke-woman." In due time, Tony the Knightly is no longer benighted, so from a cuckold to a wittol turns he. Even when divorce appears on the horizon, Tony follows Brenda's orders to take a local tart out on the town, so that Brenda can snap some photos of his supposed extracurricular escapade with the intent to bag some lifelong alimony on Tony's dime. Moreover, Tony's ancestral home is being horrendously modernized by Mrs. Beaver, John Beaver's mother, and her interior decoration techniques. Again, Tony does nothing. And it exactly because Tony temporizes with evil that he must be so heavily taxed, as he is the most gifted, of all the characters, with the capability to do good. This he pays through a brutal usurpation of his entire life.

A Handful of Dust describes what happens to those who tear down country homes with the insouciance with which they tear down all that was good and noble in the past, most notably the aesthetic sense, ideal of chivalry, and unwavering piety of Medieval Europe. This is also equally an anti-cuck novel, setting Tony up as the ultimate example of what not to do with one's life. But even more still, *A Handful of Dust* portrays what happens when one does not live a Godly life. And what is the ultimate consequence of such bad faith?

To prevent an expensive divorce, and, even more importantly, to frustrate Brenda's stealing quite a large chunk of his monthly earnings in order to lay with a few more London lads whilst her looks still last, Tony performs a cathartic release upon the reader by taking off for the Amazon Rainforest on something of a bachelor's rumpus to a find a lost city with a chief explorer and guide, Messinger. Messinger, however, gets the two lost in jungle and, rather inconveniently, dies in a canoe wreck. From there, Tony lies perishing upon the shore, experiencing over three pages' worth of uproarious hallucinations, more than a few of which include Brenda.

Moribund, Tony is approached by the mysterious Mr. Todd, who, although illiterate, owns the complete works of Charles Dickens. In return for convalescing Tony, Mr. Todd asks that Tony read Dickens to him, which request Tony is only too grateful to oblige. After returning to health, however, Tony expresses that he would like to return home to England, whereafter Mr. Todd begins to carry a shotgun during readings, never lets Tony leave the hut, and even sabotages a British rescue mission by drugging Tony and hiding him. Finally, fake news returns to England of Tony's certain death. Brenda responds by marrying Tony's attractive friend, Jock, and half of England responds by moving into Tony's former Gothic mansion turned modern carbuncle. Meanwhile, Tony rots away in the jungle, reading endlessly the works of the chronicler of Industrial Revolution—the revolution that, to date, has killed the pre-modern world for good—to a locked and loaded madman.

This leads one then to query: whither doth all this fun in the end lead us?

Waugh's *The Ordeal of Gilbert Pinfold* depicts the darkly comic nightmare of reclusive Catholic novelist and chronic insomniac Gilbert Pinfold, and his progression into the worlds of paranoia, delusion, and acute schizophrenia. Through the synthesis of a guileless, unsettlingly intimate characterization of Gilbert's neuroses, and the techniques of unreliable narration befitting of such a character, Waugh renders a surreal story about the inescapable plight of the Modern artist in middle-age. In an interview with Waugh, upon the interviewer's question as regards whether "*Pinfold* is an account of [Waugh's] own brief illness," Waugh responds with a hauntingly "Almost exact."

The novel begins with a subtle yet steadily strengthening undercurrent of latent paranoia, depicting the potential origins of Pinfold's neuroses. One's suspicions might first find arousal when one reads of Pinfold's fearful impression of "The Box." A piece of small machinery that ostensibly deals with the curing of ailments and illnesses, The Box, Pinfold opines as "An extremely dangerous device in the wrong hands," even suggesting it as "sorcery." Henceforth, the narrative becomes rapidly more self-critical, reporting that Pinfold finds "he had made no friends in late years" and concludes "he must be growing into a bore." Thereafter, one receives more insight into Pinfold's main psychological motivators: "His strongest tastes were negative. He abhorred plastics, Picasso, and jazz—everything in fact that had happened in his own lifetime." Thus far, I'm on board with Pinfold, feeling the friendship grow with each passing line.

This abhorrence for contemporary life and Romantic yearning to exist in a time other than his own are suggestive of a kind of psychological dissociation all too familiar to artists, and this notion is further bolstered by Pinfold's distant, God-like description of "his exalted point of observation," as if he himself operates detachedly in the third-person, enacting "the part(s) for which he casts himself" and becoming something of a disembodied floating eye.

One reads that Pinfold would "look at his watch and learn always with disappointment how little of his life was past, how much still lay ahead of him." The symptoms of psychological unrest pester on, as one gleans that "Mr. Pinfold slept badly" and that "For twenty-five years he had used various sedatives." Pinfold requires on "even the idlest day...six or seven hours of insensibility[,]"suggesting a strong aversion to gregariousness and other shallower versions of contemporary camaraderie.

The opening chapter closes with a B.B.C interview with Pinfold., wherein he describes the young interviewer as "commonplace...slightly sinister...accentless... [having an] insidiously plebian voice... [and] menacing," making clear his distrust and distain for the younger, blander, globalist generation. He also suggested that he can "detect in the interviewer an underlying malice." After the interview, Pinfold makes a light-hearted crack about a recently deceased celebrity whom the interviewers were next to pursue: "Cedric Thorne has escaped you. He hanged himself yesterday afternoon in his dressing-room." The interviewers are, for some reason, bothered by this brazen behavior. Pinfold ends with the claim, however, that he is "free of the fashionable agonies of *angst.*"

Waugh's quiet diatribe against Modernity's usurpation of quaint English life, although conveyed through the lens of neuroticism, does not make it a false diatribe; indeed, it is riddled with truths. This will lead more honest readers into some soul-searching as regards what a delusion truly is. Accurately described pathways into psychosis aside, *Pinfold*'s true mastery of The Paranoid is through Waugh's complete mastery of craft. Waugh illustrates said neurological diversity through prose techniques, chief of which is his subjective rendering of character interactions, of which Pinfold's neuroses completely take over all interpretation.

Pinfold's paranoia is on full display during his interactions with patrons aboard the SS Caliban. He is constantly misinterpreting the words, thoughts, and indeed entire demeanors of everyone with whom he interacts. In an interaction with a woman who yesterday much enjoyed the conversation she had with Pinfold, Pinfold continues thusly: "I'm afraid I was an awful bore last night... All that nonsense I talked... I shan't hold forth like that again." To which, the woman responds, "Not while you were with us...I was fascinated...Please do." Pinfold overhears further imaginary conversations in which he is discussed as a drinker and as addicted to sleeping pills—all such conversations taking on a sinister and accusatory manner.

Pinfold often reports auditory hallucinations that occur in his personal compartment aboard The SS Caliban. His hallucinations there, which he claims to hear through the wires or the vents, range from hearing a priest strongly reprimanding a boy for having "pictures of girls stuck up by [his] bunk," to the unforgettable *hooligans* who threaten to "wait until he's asleep...

then...pounce," call him "a Jew," and therefore the apt "Mr. Peinfeld." It is also through the vents that Pinfold also takes part in a marriage ceremony between his doppelgänger and young girl named Margaret.

Pinfold's interpretations are ludicrous, and the readerly effect thereof is very enjoyable. Moreover, the scenes are quite effective on readers due to their preying on foibles about which many people become paranoid from time to time, perhaps leading one to connect deeply with Pinfold, a character one might perceive as insane.

The Ordeal of Gilbert Pinfold portrays an honest delusion: modern paranoia. Yet, far from pulp sensationalism or tales of The Strange, *Pinfold* seeks to record what T.S. Eliot considered the most important thing each generation of literature could pursue: to find that era's realism. It seems that the best way to convey some truth in today's world is to abstain from suggesting rational, ethical, sane characters as being the best representatives for both individual psychology and common personality at large. It is likely more honest to posit that today's modern denizens share more in common with insomniacs, paranoids, and neurotics, share more with people like Gilbert Pinfold. Above all, however, *The Ordeal of Gilbert Pinfold* is Waugh's haunting promise of the inevitability of the artist's mind: with each passing hour, one hears growing louder the devil's laughter.

Waugh's over thirty-five-year diasporic odyssey with wit can be likewise keenly observed throughout his *Complete Short Stories*, starting, perchance, with his 1930 short story "The Manager of "'The Kremlin.'" Boris, a wandering defector of the Russian military, is described as "ill-dressed and friendless, in another strange city...lost in a wasteland, patrolled by enemy troops and inhabited by savage(s)." The additional allusion to T.S. Eliot's poem about the rootlessness of Modernity, *The Wasteland* (also quoted at the beginning of *A Handful of Dust*), and the character's being lastly depicted as having "lost one's country," serve as further flicks to the ear.

"Love in the Slump" describes one man's experience in a strange part of the English countryside after a horseback hunting accident as awaking "quite alone in a totally strange country." "Out of depth" contains a more blatant reference to this theme in its fitting character, Rip, and his surreal encounter with occult visions of a dark, dystopian future:

> *The officers and officials came and went. There was a talk of sending him "home." Home, thought Rip and beyond the next official town, vague and more distant, he saw the orderly succession of characterless, steam-heated apartments, the cabin trunks and promenade decks, the casinos and bars and supper restaurants that were his home...*

"The Man Who Liked Dickens" follows a man who, after a failed African expedition, is marooned and held captive by a local madman, and therefore entirely without the possibility of return to his English home (the ending from *A Handful of Dust*). Similar themes can be gleaned in "On Guard", wherein a young husband is rendered unable, on account of a lengthy and failing African farming endeavor, to return to both England and his unfaithful wife. Related themes, such as leaving one's intellectual home by way of daydreaming, can be found as well throughout the collection, suggesting each character's difficulties with this special kind of cognitive dissonance as concomitant to the phenomenon of the loss of the Home.

Yet, it is exactly this kind of cerebral eccentricity that is necessary for the development of wit. Just as one must, whenever without a home in the world, devise an intellectual hovel for oneself, does wit's roguish associative logic develop. Wit may not indulge; it must remain entirely phlegmatic in its flitting, lest it take an unironic stance, and with this pious misstep lose all of its fleetfooted secularity. Wit makes a deliberate end of its interminable process, and, in this way, makes a puckish home of its inherent homelessness.

Vladimir Nabokov

THE TALE OF TWO STORIES

It would not be too much to say that Vladimir Nabokov was a gentleman of opinions. According to Nabokov, modern psychology was preposterous; Hemingway was essentially a writer for young boys; Albert Camus: puffed-up, ephemeral, second-rate; Oscar Wilde: a rank moralist; James Joyce: an unparalleled genius. And women (aside from his wife, Vera) were not to have any hand in the editing of his work. Such a personality might also be considered preposterous, if it were not for Nabokov's writing being so splendid.

Nabokov believed a good writer to possess the precision of a poet and the imagination of a scientist. Of a good reader, Nabokov proposed that she should possess four main things: an imagination, a memory, some artistic sense, and, much to the dismay of today's four-letter readers: a dictionary. The origins concerning this damn matter are up for conjecture, but it is nevertheless common practice that the modern reader often scoffs at one's employment of a vast vocabulary as mere vague pretension, lexical posturing, or etymological dick-measuring. The modern reader is envious. Nabokov's vocabulary was—good—and the subsequent labyrinth of poetic texture created therewith in his novel *Lolita,* enchanting. Secure philologists the world over swoon at his prose's ability to infinitely charm, to every time regale those good Nabokovian readers with the perfect word and a tale of (at least) two simultaneous stories.

To some, *Lolita* is a story about a heaving, vulgar pedophile lusting for the fruits of an innocent and helpless child. Please forgive them; the public-school system is soon due for reform. Nonetheless, any way one ogles at it, the novel is certainly amorous in tone. But, nearly completely naked of any description of true fornication, the book subtly presents to the reader a beautiful moral dilemma: we understand Humbert; we are sympathetic towards him; we are also hot and bothered. But that's wrong, right?

One way of many Nabokov gets us petting heavy at otherwise commonplace scenes regarding quotidian endeavors is through connotation. In today's highly poetic world, with such understated masterpieces as "the horizontal boogie," or "checking the plumbing," in order to "clean the pipes," innuendo and double entendre have obviously reached levels of an almost perfect art. Yet, despite the odds of ever becoming any more subtle than the aforementioned, Nabokov erects connotation to a new climax. Engorged senses become "full to the brim," and sudden commotions "prevent() them from overflowing," after which there are "aching veins." "Gay dogs...unload...career girls" onto the dashing Humbert. Humbert is "moved" by Lolita's "slangy speech." And when Humbert plays with the idea of becoming Lolita's father, he is certain that "if all of (his) troubles would be expelled; (he) would be a healthy man." It is almost as if Nabokov planned all those words to be where they are, as if he were trying to say two things at once.

Whether we like it or not, our names have a lot to do with our identity. Joshes are good at breaking down walls. Davids are good with slings. Smiths make our tools. Bakers make us fat. Geoffrey Chaucer is widely credited with the first use of meaningful names in English literature, insofar as the names he devised for his characters referred, whether satirically or not, to some occupation, dominant personality trait, or connection that he or she might have with the budding Western Literary Canon. Nabokov continues this tradition. Consider Dr. Blanche Schwarzmann, a name Nabokov uses to satirize the standard psychologist; here, Nabokov reminds us that modern psychology retains a myopically black (German: Schwarz) and white (French: blanche) assertion towards the meaning to consciousness and all the contents pertaining thereto. And what about Nabokov's creation in Ms. Phalen (failing), the "old spinster." Indeed, choosing the right name for a character is as important as the words chosen to describe them thereafter.

The God of all double storytelling is allusion. The allusion is an immensely powerful tool for the lexically inclined and is indeed the king of subtle wit, as it requires a deep understanding of not only the text at hand, but also of various other texts and their many relations to that text at hand; this is the beautiful bower to which all writers and readers should strive. Nabokov, much like one of his favorite writers, James Joyce, writes much of his books almost entirely in allusion. There can be, by using this method, quite literally two, three, four, perhaps infinite stories happening at once. *Lolita*'s phony foreword by the phony professor John Ray refers to Humbert Humbert (H.H. Holmes?) through the phrase of "he is not a gentleman," an allusion to James

Joyce's *Ulysses*'s opening chapter, and the character Buck Mulligan's wrongful instigation of Stephen Daedalus. Shakespeare's *Romeo and Juliet* takes the stage with the staging of Humbert's childhood romance with Annabel in "a kind of cave" by the beach, after which failed encounter she dies, and so does childhood and the feeling of love for Humbert; he is forever in love with that child(hood): Humbert's a Romantic. What about the frequent comparisons of Lolita to that Mother of Humanity, Eve? Nabokov compares Lolita to Annabel and his childhood beach romance as that "immortal" day. Lolita eats "Eden-red apple(s)" and "immemorial fruit." When canoodling with Lolita on the couch he states that the interaction "would suffice to set all paradise loose," which is also a nice usage of innuendo, whereupon Humbert goes upstairs to shower in a "deluge of steaming water," nicely intimating the diluvial flood, as well as the baptism, and furthermore the Rebirth; Humbert has been reborn into Eden.

Words are at their most beautiful when they have many stories to tell, and *Lolita* is, for those interested in lexical beauty, a most attractive work to behold, perhaps, in the world of aesthetics, a perfect ten. Nabokov is a master linguist who leaves his prose prodding, pinging, and prickling around in the minds of all appreciative readers. Humbert, condemned to a psychiatric ward, asks us, pleads us to "look at this tangle of thorns."

Oscar Wilde

ANTITHESIS WILDE

One cannot go on too long about the subject of wit and not mention everyone's favorite fop.

Oscar Wilde was a dandy, and everyone hated him for it. He sported a flower in his buttonhole, enjoyed a good bacchanalian night out on the town, and was a firm fan of the love that dare not speak its name. A stark proponent of art for art's sake and aesthetics as the paragon of creative expression, Wilde was, purportedly, not very much into telling chaps what to do or how to do it. Victorian England, however, was chock-full of fellows telling other gents how to do things the right way, and Wilde, in the eyes of Victorian moralists, could do only wrong. But moralists, though often competent gaolers, never make for good writers. Therefore, it is fitting that Wilde, the amoral contrarian and talented poet, playwright, and prose-artist (and later prisoner), was particularly fond of a form of rhetoric called Antithesis. Indeed, much of Wilde's flamboyantly aphoristic writing style is due to his almost suffocating employment of this quipping form, performing it, in fact, so often that he immortalized himself in the rhetorical world by way of the Wildean Antithesis.

Antithesis is whenever one constructs a statement and then connects another directly thereafter that is in general opposition for the first, serving as an equal and reverse lexical comparison to some interesting new posited insight. In this way, an antithesis creates a kind of mellifluous dialectic insofar as it presents a thesis (New Insight: X is Y), an antithesis (Negation or Reaction: not X is not Y), and a synthesis: an appealing merger of two ideas creating a highly satisfying semblance of poetic logic.

Antithesis comes off as incredibly witty, yet also as incredibly cute. This is dangerous, as Cuteness (and her hotter sister, Irony), does have the propensity to become annoying or grow tired and should thus be flirted with judiciously. However, unlike the complex, arduous mating-dance required of Irony, Antithesis is easy. Wilde knew this and, as a man unafraid to, perchance, fag out his readers, chanced to woo her any and every chance he got, sometimes an immortal four or five times per page.

Here is how he did it in his novel *The Picture of Dorian Gray*: "Nothing can cure the soul but the senses" ...(Assertion)," just as nothing can cure the senses but the soul" (Contrary Assertion). This is an example of a rather straightforward premise/negation antithetical configuration that creates that edifyingly chin-scratching juxtaposition so often sought after by writers. But then Wilde goes wild, hitting us again not a hundred words later with an antithesis of almost identical construction: "You know more than you think you know, just as you know less than you want to know." But did you see what he did there? As rhetoric is, much to the benefit of the sensible world, not logic, one is allowed to tweak one's antithesis to appeal not only to computers, rather also to humans; instead of insulting his readers by comparing thinking with thinking, Wilde compares thinking *against* wanting, a comparison much more apt to the logic of Humanity.

In addition to a witty rhetorical scheme, a good antithesis is a great way to be remembered. *The Picture of Dorian Gray* contains two of Wilde's most oft-quoted antitheses, both of which pertain to his favorite subject: Men—and one to his least favorite—Women. *Gray*'s arguably fictional character, Lord Harry, also thinks very little of women, for he states that "Women represent the triumph of matter over mind, just as men represent the triumph of mind over morals," just as Wilde's other rejoining talking-head, Uncle George, thinks very little of ungentle men: "if a man is a gentleman, he knows quite enough, and if he is not a gentleman, whatever he knows is bad for him." Wilde did find other occasions outside of *Gray* to provide his obviously personal opinions about Man and The Other One Made of His Rib—that ineluctable binary that is still the most easily discernable antithesis known to Humankind.

For example, his stylish misogyny is likewise not lost in such romantic epigrams as "A man's face is his autobiography. A woman's face is her work of fiction," or "How can a woman be expected to be happy with a man who insists on treating her as if she were a perfectly normal human being?" But Wilde is, in the end, willing to spread the butter evenly: "All women become like their mothers. That is their tragedy. No man does. That's his." Indeed, whatever one's opinion on the sexes and their relation to gentleness, truthfulness, or mothers might be, if it be in one's interest to deceive others with the appearance of being knowledgeable and cultured, it is best to say or write whatever nonsense one might conjure in the form of an antithesis.

At the beginning of this essay, Wilde was described as generally amoral, and someone without the desire to oppress his opinion on others. In truth, however, there is no more judgmental a man upon the printed page, no more eager a man to tell another that he has got it the wrong way around. He merely puts it in the opposite way that most would; that is, he says it in the form of an antithesis. Let us investigate Wilde's thoughts on a few other topics to check on the validity of this claim.

Normally, friends are quite happy to help each other, can be trusted with relative ease, and bring one another a deep sense of happiness and meaning. We revel in the successes of our friends, because, as they mean so much to us, their successes feel like our successes. Enemies, on the other hand, are there to present problems, fill us with anxiety, dread, or fear, and are generally interested in our downfall. Aside from the fact that most people do not have enemies, as these are more often referred to a managers, the above description is a description of relationships in the normal world. In Wilde's world, however, things work a touch differently: "It is very easy to endure the difficulties of one's enemies. It is the successes of one's friends that are hard to bear." Similarly, for Wilde, the idea of happiness itself presents enough ambiguity for the following antithesis: "There are only two tragedies in life: one is not getting what one wants, and the other is getting it." Thus, friends and happiness are equally undesirable, leaving us in the very capable hands of managers and misery. Of course, it is but only a conjecture by the Humble Writer of these pages, but I should wager that these two beliefs might have contributed to his third: "Some cause happiness wherever they go; others whenever they go."

Forsooth, it matters not in what topic that one might have interest—Wilde has an antithesis for it.

Money?

> *When I was young I thought that money was the most important thing in life; now that I am old I know that it is.*

Fame?

> *There is only one thing in life worse than being talked about, and that is not being talked about.*

Wit?

> *Sarcasm is the lowest form of wit, but the highest form of intelligence.*

The man is indeed one bump into the solid edge of an open door away from being a fortune cookie. How does Wilde, who essentially preaches and personifies Cole Porter's classic "Everything Goes," have so many recommendations about how things should be? The explanation for this is elementary.

Contrarianism, if it were poured into a mixer and served cold in a glass, would taste the same as having a personality that defies anything that it encounters; thus, Wilde, contrarianism incarnate, has so many things to say precisely because he does not have a position, besides that of being always against the one presently in place.

The number of serious thinkers and hot bags of air who fit into this category are legion, and it seems to be, amongst the endless platoons of variables that may be influencing said thinkers and airbags, that a distain for authority be the common streak. Wilde was not, aside from his never actually directly stating his feelings on the matter, shy about his stating his feelings on that matter. Rightfully, some people allow the writing to speak for itself. Wilde, though, prefers to let it scream. That said, I am in firm disagreement with Wilde's suggestion that "An idea that is not dangerous is unworthy of being called an idea at all," but I am nevertheless sympathetic to his contrarian sentiments.

And that is the thing, really. One need not have the correct opinion about anything to be witty, rather the opinion in question must be so agreeably turned that it does not matter what the correct opinion is, for the witty opinion is striking, memorable, and therefore taken as gospel.

Is Wilde, for instance, destined to win the favor of any state or national school boards with this terrifically tuned zinger? "Education is an admirable thing. But it is well to remember from time to time that nothing that is worth knowing can be taught." What about the Church with this contribution to the good fight? "It is absurd to divide people into good and bad. People are either charming or tedious." My conclusion, on both counts, leans away from the affirmative. In a similar vein, it is purely a hunch of mine that Wilde would have likely thought himself an excellent man; therefore, the opinions of his friends would, obviously, be out: "an excellent man; he has no enemies; and none of his friends like him." Again, this is but a hunch, but the notion weights heavy on me that it would have likely been a trifle difficult to have been a good friend of Wilde's.

Nay, for you cannot be right: "Consistency is the last refuge of the unimaginative." You may not be serious: "Life is too much important a thing ever to talk seriously about it." And, according to Wilde, you are not even allowed to be yourself: "Most people are other people. Their thoughts are someone else's opinions, their life a mimicry, their passions a quotation." Furthermore, were one, for one reason or another, to be in accordance with these ideas of his, then Wilde would likewise deem you a puzzlepated dunderheaded: "Ah! Don't say you agree with me. When people agree with me I always feel that I must be wrong." Amongst the multiple interpretations herein suggested, two are certainties. One: Oscar Wilde is a phenomenal Wit. Two: to have been in the regular society of Mr. Wilde must have been, on a good day, exhausting.

Oscar Wilde, (in)famous popinjay, flaneur, and homosexual, was himself the antithesis to the Victorian world. It is up to interpretation, then, with his divinely symbolic death in 1900, that he remains either the eternal, tragic bedfellow of Queen Victoria, or rather ushered in the even more tragic, but oh-so-Wildean, 20th century. If Wilde would have lived to see the Roaring Twenties and beyond, however, he would have been just another gallivanting dandy amongst many; and, something tells me that, once he would have realized that he was in the Majority, he would have become the most conservative Anglican British Loyalist Imperialist Tory of any Irishman in history.

G.K. Chesterton

THE PATER OF PARADOX

But who is the antithesis to Oscar Wilde?

G.K. Chesterton remarked that "carpe diem is not the religion of happy people, but of very unhappy people" and that Oscar Wilde was married to this "desolate philosophy." Wilde was a thrall to the "cult of the pessimistic pleasure-seeker" and strove tirelessly to get us to be as miserable as he. "Oscar Wilde said that sunsets were not valued because we could not pay for sunsets," writes Chesterton in his 1908 chef d'oeuvre, *Orthodoxy*. However, Chesterton goes on to suggest otherwise: "Wilde was wrong; we can pay for sunsets. We can pay for them by not being Oscar Wilde." Yet, despite the very lucrative business that Chesterton could have made out of handsomely dragging Wilde's legacy through the Augean Stable, he chose not to—opting instead for offering all of humanity a plush, new, white terry cloth with which to muck out the stalls.

It is hard to write about Chesterton, for one comes to the conclusion that the best way to write about Chesterton is to tell the reader to go out and buy a Chesterton. He is perhaps one of the most quotable, if not the most quotable, of all authors I have ever read; his veritable torrent of quips, maxims, and epigrams leave one sore in the chops and rummaging around for the jaw kerchief. Ultimately, Chesterton is the balance to Wilde. He is the rotund, chortling saint that keeps wildness in order. Whereas Wilde, high priest of the unorthodox, undertook his philosophy with great rigidity and repetition, Chesterton, the ultimate apologetic to orthodoxy, flourished greatly by the protean state of his child-like mind. This is a very paradoxical state of affairs, which, paradoxically, works as a fitting transition into one of the most important conceptions at the very core of wit: paradox.

A paradox, if you want some of the all-encapsulating stuff, is something like a seemingly absurd, contradictory, and logically self-contradictory statement or proposition that runs contrary to one's expectations yet, whenever investigated, proves to be well founded or true. Known as the Price of Paradox, Chesterton lived hugely up to his sobriquet and was sometimes even ridiculed by lesser thinkers for churning out dressed-up doggerel: "Mere light sophistry is the thing that I happen to despise most of all things, and it is perhaps a wholesome fact that this is the thing of which I am generally accused. I know nothing so contemptible as a mere paradox; a mere ingenious defence of the indefensible."

Far from producing merely weightless turns of phrase, Chesterton's nearly 300-pound body supported the sizable head that was in the business of heavyweight ideas: "If he asks me why I introduce what he calls paradoxes into a philosophical problem, I answer, because all philosophical problems tend to become paradoxical." It might seem paradoxical but spending as much time thinking in paradox as possible is the best way to come to finite and reliable conclusions. Thinking about, or even solving, paradoxes aids us in being in control of our own ideas and helps us in avoiding the extremes of thought, for, to embrace a paradox is to embrace contradictory ideas, which leads to the ability to conceive, contend, and ultimately balance multiple antitheses simultaneously.

Indeed, put it to the test, and you will find that mental mavericks of all stripes spend considerable time in this exact balance of thought, for this balancing of paradoxical notions, paradoxically, leads to stunning clarity of mind, as "The man of no ideas," Chesterton notes, "will find the first idea fly to his head like wine to the head of a teetotaller." This sciamachy with many ostensibly irreconcilable cognitive opponents eventually leads one to becoming their master, as Chesterton writes, "Ideas are dangerous, but the man to whom they are least dangerous is the man of ideas. He is acquainted with ideas, and moves among them like a lion-tamer."

For the learning of an art form, I have little doubt that a light dash of theory followed by an outright onslaught of examples is the way of champions. Therefore, without further ado, I present a mere portion of a subfraction of a fraction of the paradoxes of G.K. Chesterton.

On Orthodoxy:

Chesterton was an Anglican for most of his life, until his converted to Catholicism 1922. At either stage of his religious life, however, Chesterton was a firm proponent of orthodoxy, which, in addition to religious implications, also denotes an authorized or generally accepted theory, doctrine, or practice. In Chesterton's astute observation, "Nothing more strangely indicates an enormous and silent evil of modern society than the extraordinary use which is made nowadays of the word "orthodox." In former days the heretic was proud of not being a heretic." As regards revolution, both of the social and the spiritual kind, he was of the firm opinion that it was a behavior of perverted vanity and served only the purpose of getting further and further away from contentment and Truth.

> *The word "orthodoxy" not only no longer means being right; it practically means being wrong. All this can mean one thing, and one thing only. It means that people care less for whether they are philosophically right.*

> *Atheism itself is too theological for us to-day. Revolution itself is too much of a system; liberty itself is too much of a restraint.*

> *Never has there been so little discussion about the nature of men as now, when, for the first time, any one can discuss it. The old restriction meant that only the orthodox were allowed to discuss religion. Modern liberty means that nobody is allowed to discuss it.*

> *Orthodoxy is not only (as is often urged) the only safe guardian of morality or order, but is also the only logical guardian of liberty, innovation and advance.*

> *When everything about a people is for the time growing weak and ineffective, it begins to talk about efficiency. So it*

is that when a man's body is a wreck he begins, for the first time, to talk about health.

He may even go mad; but he is going mad for the love of sanity. But the modern student of ethics, even if he remains sane, remains sane from an insane dread of insanity.

This is the thrilling romance of Orthodoxy. People have fallen into a foolish habit of speaking of orthodoxy as something heavy, humdrum, and safe. There never was anything so perilous or so exciting as orthodoxy.

It is only since I have known orthodoxy that I have known mental emancipation.

On Being Smaller:

There are many today who believe in the untenable cliché of *expand your horizons.* If one were to take a moment to think about horizons, however, the impossibility of that task becomes clear, for the horizon remains exactly that: the limits to what we can see. That is determined by the curvature of the earth and the obstacles on the skyline. Man was never meant to see far. But man is uncannily good at seeing things closely. He excels with high honors at becoming intimate with his immediate surroundings, learning their every subtlety, and then writing myths about them. All else is merely a vacation.

The globe-trotter lives in a smaller world than the peasant.

The truth is that exploration and enlargement make the world smaller. The telegraph and the steamboat make the world smaller. The telescope makes the world smaller; it is only the microscope that makes it larger.

We have to love our neighbour because he is there... He is the sample of humanity which is actually given us. Precisely because he may be anybody he is everybody. He is a symbol because he is an accident

The man standing in his own kitchen-garden, with fairyland opening at the gate, is the man with large ideas.

Doubtless men flee from small environments into lands that are very deadly. But this is natural enough; for they are not fleeing from death. They are fleeing from life.

It is quite proper that a British diplomatist should seek the society of Japanese generals, if what he wants is Japanese generals. But if what he wants is people different from himself, he had much better stop at home and discuss religion with the housemaid.

On Being Innocent of the Fact:

The fact that anything happens to anyone at all is because he did not expect it to happen. Surely, expected things could happen or occur to someone who was waiting for it with a Louisville Slugger, but that does not make it a happening or an occurrence. Much as one cannot learn without new information, tire without expending effort, or laugh without feeling tickled, one cannot see without looking; or, as Hermetic philosophy puts it, "The lips of Wisdom are closed, except to the ears of Understanding."

The one supreme way of making all those processes go right, the processes of health, and strength, and grace, and beauty, the one and only way of making certain of their accuracy, is to think about something else.

The man who expects nothing sees redder roses than common men can see, and greener grass, and a more startling sun.

Until we realize that things might not be we cannot realize that things are. Until we see the background of darkness we cannot admire the light as a single and created thing. As soon as we have seen that darkness, all light is lightening, sudden, blinding, and divine.

As long as a tree is a tree, it is a top-heavy monster with a hundred arms, a thousand tongues, and only one leg. But so long as a tree is a tree, it does not frighten us at all. It begins to be something alien, to be something strange, only when it looks like ourselves. When a tree really looks like a man our knees knock under us. And when the whole universe looks like a man we fall on our faces.

Take away the supernatural, and what remains is the unnatural.

They are becoming conscious of their own strength—that is, they are growing weaker.

Adventures are to those to whom they are most unexpected—that is, most romantic. Adventures are to the shy: in this sense adventures are to the unadventurous.

The food will really renovate his tissues as long as he is not thinking about his tissues. The exercise will really get him into training so long as he is thinking about something else. And the marriage will really stand some chance of producing a generous-blooded generation if it had its origin in its own natural and generous excitement. It is the first law of health that our necessities should not be accepted as necessities; they should be accepted as luxuries.

The strong cannot be brave. Only the weak can be brave; and yet again, in practice, only those who can be brave can be trusted, in time of doubt, to be strong.

He must surely see that the fact of two things being different implies that they are similar.

On Madness and Sanity:

As more and more people today qualify as "mad," this leads one to something of a fork in the road. Off the left-hand side of the path, there is a parallel river that flows to a great body of water, from which the large populace drinks deeply and often. The entirety of this water-source is contaminated, but its many drinkers report no negative effects—though only because everyone is too demented to notice them. This, as one might imagine, is an unlikely scenario. On the right-hand side of the river, there is a beautiful trail that leads to a modern office building. In this office building, unimportant people do important things. One of those things is deciding what constitutes a demented person. The main thing to remember here is that everyone in this office building is insane. Now, this scenario happens every day.

> *There is a notion adrift everywhere that imagination, especially mystical imagination, is dangerous to man's mental balance. Poets are commonly spoken of as psychologically unreliable; and generally there is a vague association between wreathing laurels in your hair and sticking straws in it. Facts and history utterly contradict this view. Most of the very great poets have been not only sane, but extremely business-like; and if Shakespeare ever really held horses, it was because he was much the safest man to hold them. Imagination does not breed insanity. Exactly what does breed insanity is reason. Poets do not go mad; but chess-players do. Mathematicians go mad, and cashiers; but creative artists very seldom. I am not, as will be seen, in any sense attacking logic: I only say that this danger does lie in logic, not in imagination.*
>
> *It is true that some speak lightly and loosely of insanity as in itself attractive. But a moment's thought will show that if disease is beautiful, it is generally some one else's disease. A blind man may be picturesque; but it requires two eyes to see the picture. And similarly even the wildest poetry of*

insanity can only be enjoyed by the sane. To the insane man his insanity is quite prosaic, because it is quite true.

It would be much truer to say that a man will certainly fail, because he believes in himself. Complete self-confidence is not merely a sin; complete self-confidence is a weakness.

Oddities only strike ordinary people. Oddities do not strike odd people. This is why ordinary people have a much more exciting time; while odd people are always complaining of the dulness of life.

The general fact is simple. Poetry is sane because it floats easily in an infinite sea; reason seeks to cross the infinite sea, and so make it finite.

If you argue with a madman, it is extremely probable that you will get the worst of it; for in many ways his mind moves all the quicker for not being delayed by the things that go with good judgment. He is not hampered by a sense of humour or by charity, or by the dumb certainties of experience. He is the more logical for losing certain sane affections. Indeed, the common phrase for insanity is in this respect a misleading one. The madman is not the man who has lost his reason. The madman is the man who has lost everything except his reason.

The strongest and most unmistakable MARK of madness is this combination between a logical completeness and a spiritual contraction. The lunatic's theory explains a large number of things, but it does not explain them in a large way.

The sane man knows that he has a touch of the beast, a touch of the devil, a touch of the saint, a touch of the citizen. Nay, the really sane man knows that he has a touch of the madman. But the materialist's world is quite simple and solid, just as the madman is quite sure he is sane. The materialist is sure that history has been simply and solely a chain of causation...Materialists and madmen never have doubts.

The man who cannot believe his senses, and the man who cannot believe anything else, are both insane, but their insanity is proved not by any error in their argument, but by the manifest mistake of their whole lives.

Mysticism keeps men sane. As long as you have mystery you have health; when you destroy mystery you create morbidity.

On the Artist and the Artistic Temperament:

Anyone who is trying to convince you of any group aspect of art, or, worse yet, actively asking you to participate in the creation of art in groups with other artists, is either trying to sell you a car that you do not want or, as in the latter case, trying to frogmarch you onto the crowded public bus, with your pants at your ankles, by calling it a Ferrari. Art has always been a solitary endeavor; any art worth experiencing was ultimately filtered through the mind of a single brilliant individual. And that brilliant individual either refused to take full credit, gave glory unto God, or remained anonymous. At the very least, he did not look, talk, or act like an Artist.

When Byron divided humanity into the bores and bored, he omitted to notice that the higher qualities exist entirely in the bores, the lower qualities in the bored, among whom he counted himself. The bore, by his starry enthusiasm, his solemn happiness, may, in some sense, have proved himself poetical. The bored has certainly proved himself prosaic.

Any man with a vital knowledge of the human psychology ought to have the most profound suspicion of anybody who claims to be an artist, and talks a great deal about art. Art is a right and human thing, like walking or saying one's prayers; but the moment it begins to be talked about very solemnly, a man may be fairly certain that the thing has come into a congestion and a kind of difficulty.

Artists of a large and wholesome vitality get rid of their art easily, as they breathe easily, or perspire easily. But in artists of less force, the thing becomes a pressure, and produces a definite pain, which is called the artistic temperament.

It need hardly be said that this is the real explanation of the thing which has puzzled so many dilettante critics, the problem of the extreme ordinariness of the behaviour of so many great geniuses in history. Their behaviour was so ordinary that it was not recorded; hence it was so ordinary that it seemed mysterious. Hence people say that Bacon wrote Shakespeare. The modern artistic temperament cannot understand how a man who could write such lyrics as Shakespeare wrote, could be as keen as Shakespeare was on business transactions in a little town in Warwickshire. The explanation is simple enough; it is that Shakespeare had a real lyrical impulse, wrote a real lyric, and so got rid of the impulse and went about his business. Being an artist did not prevent him from being an ordinary man, any more than being a sleeper at night or being a diner at dinner prevented him from being an ordinary man.

Anarchism adjures us to be bold creative artists, and care for no laws or limits. But it is impossible to be an artist and not care for laws and limits. Art is limitation; the essence of every picture is the frame.

The artist loves his limitations: they constitute the THING he is doing. The painter is glad that the canvas is flat. The sculptor is glad that the clay is colourless.

On Nietzsche:

Honey is a deliciously sweet treacle that one may enjoy in tea, on desserts, or simply by the spoonful. Honey is also used to catch flies. This is called a honey-trap. At first, the fly thinks that the honey is the greatest thing in the world; it is the most amazing thing that the fly has ever seen! Upon swooping down and sipping the ambrosia, the fly is then convinced that he is in possession of something special and that all else who spurn it are fools. Soon thereafter, the fly finds that he cannot move. The honey has a hold of him. His efforts become more and more futile, until his head finally goes under, and he drowns on the nectar that, he thought, gave him so much life. To Chesterton, Nietzsche is much like this.

> *If Nietzsche had not ended in imbecility, Nietzscheism would end in imbecility. Thinking in isolation and with pride ends in being an idiot. Every man who will not have softening of the heart must at last have softening of the brain.*

> *The worship of will is the negation of will. To admire mere choice is to refuse to choose...All the will-worshippers, from Nietzsche to Mr. Davidson, are really quite empty of volition.*

> *We may say broadly that free thought is the best of all the safeguards against freedom. Managed in a modern style the emancipation of the slave's mind is the best way of preventing the emancipation of the slave. Teach him to worry about whether he wants to be free, and he will not free himself...He is too mentally worried to believe in freedom. He is kept quiet with revolutionary literature. He is calmed and kept in his place by a constant succession of wild philosophies. He is a Marxian one day, a Nietzscheite the next day, a Superman (probably) the next day; and a slave every day.*

> *I can see the inevitable smash of the philosophies of Schopenhauer and Tolstoy, Nietzsche and Shaw, as clearly*

as an inevitable railway smash could be seen from a balloon. They are all on the road to the emptiness of the asylum. For madness may be defined as using mental activity so as to reach mental helplessness; and they have nearly reached it.

Nietzsche scales staggering mountains, but he turns up ultimately in Tibet.

On Christianity and Its Values:

Christianity, Chesterton would have said, is the ultimate paradox, because, in Christianity, one is required to think and live in total paradox. In this way, Christianity most closely mirrors life and all its experiences; therefore, Christianity is to be studied, understood, and lived. For, any other mode of life, according to Chesterton, would be simply madness.

The sages, it is often said, can see no answer to the riddle of religion. But the trouble with our sages is not that they cannot see the answer; it is that they cannot even see the riddle. They are like children so stupid as to notice nothing paradoxical in the playful assertion that a door is not a door.

Christianity is a superhuman paradox whereby two opposite passions may blaze beside each other.

Charity is a paradox, like modesty and courage. Stated baldly, charity certainly means one of two things—pardoning unpardonable acts, or loving unlovable people.

Courage is almost a contradiction in terms. It means a strong desire to live taking the form of a readiness to die. "He that will lose his life, the same shall save it," is not a piece of mysticism for saints and heroes. It is a piece of everyday advice for sailors or mountaineers. It might be printed in an Alpine guide or a drill book. This paradox is the whole principle of courage; even of quite earthly or quite brutal courage. A man cut off by the sea may save his life if he will risk it on the precipice... He can only get away from death by continually stepping within an inch of it. A soldier surrounded by enemies, if he is to cut his way out, needs to combine a strong desire for living with a strange carelessness about dying.

How can man be approximately free of fine emotions, able to swing them in a clear space without breakage or wrong? THIS was the achievement of this Christian paradox of the parallel passions. Granted the primary dogma of the war between divine and diabolic, the revolt and ruin of the world, their optimism and pessimism, as pure poetry, could be loosened like cataracts.

But all conservatism is based upon the idea that if you leave things alone you leave them as they are. But you do not. If you leave a thing alone you leave it to a torrent of change. If you leave a white post alone it will soon be a black post. If you particularly want it to be white you must be always painting it again; that is, you must be always having a revolution. Briefly, if you want the old white post you must have a new white post. But this which is true even of inanimate things is in a quite special and terrible sense true of all human things. An almost unnatural vigilance is really required of the citizen because of the horrible rapidity with which human institutions grow old. It is the custom in passing romance and journalism to talk of men suffering under old tyrannies. But, as a fact, men have almost always suffered under new tyrannies; under tyrannies that had been public liberties hardly twenty years before.

We talk of wild animals; but man is the only wild animal. It is man that has broken out. All other animals are tame animals; following the rugged respectability of the tribe or type. All other animals are domestic animals; man alone is ever undomestic, either as a profligate or a monk. So that this first superficial reason for materialism is, if anything, a reason for its opposite; it is exactly where biology leaves off that all religion begins.

Of course the family is a good institution because it is uncongenial. It is wholesome precisely because it contains so many divergencies and varieties.

It is not merely true that the age which has settled least what is progress is this "progressive" age. It is, moreover, true that the people who have settled least what is progress are the most "progressive" people in it. The ordinary mass, the men who have never troubled about progress, might be trusted perhaps to progress. The particular individuals who talk about progress would certainly fly to the four winds of heaven when the pistol-shot started the race...Progress is not an illegitimate word, but it is logically evident that it is illegitimate for us. It is a sacred word, a word which could only rightly be used by rigid believers and in the ages of faith.

If the change-worshipper wishes to estimate his own progress, he must be sternly loyal to the ideal of change; he must not begin to flirt gaily with the ideal of monotony. Progress itself cannot progress.

The modern man can hardly get away from ritual except by entering a ritualistic church.

It is we Christians who accept all actual evidence—it is you rationalists who refuse actual evidence being constrained to do so by your creed.

On Laughter, Jokes, Humor, Happiness, Mirth, and Wit:

G.K. Chesterton's was an intellect of supremely untrammeled wit. While his paradoxes indubitably portray a depth, breadth, and exactness of thinking that is truly intimidating, his chief exercise is that of a humorist. Lighthearted and wholesome merrymaking was his stock and trade, and the humorous temperament, both he and The Humble Author agree, was something in service of the divine. "For a hearty laugh," Chesterton rightly observed, "it is necessary to have touched the heart."

To take a thing and make a joke out of it is not to take it in vain. It is, on the contrary, to take it and use it for an uncommonly good object. To use a thing in vain means to use it without use.

The thing which is fundamentally and really frivolous is not a careless joke. The thing which is fundamentally and really frivolous is a careless solemnity.

About what other subjects can one make jokes except serious subjects? It is quite useless to talk about profane jesting. All jesting is in its nature profane, in the sense that it must be the sudden realization that something which thinks itself solemn is not so very solemn after all.

Men talk for hours with the faces of a college of cardinals about things like golf, or tobacco, or waistcoats, or party politics. But all the most grave and dreadful things in the world are the oldest jokes in the world—being married; being hanged.

Once men sang together round a table in chorus; now one man sings alone, for the absurd reason that he can sing better. If scientific civilization goes on (which is most improbable) only one man will laugh, because he can laugh better than the rest.

There are three distinct classes of great satirists who are also great men—that is to say, three classes of men who can laugh at something without losing their souls. The satirist of the first type is the man who, first of all enjoys himself, and then enjoys his enemies...There is a second type of mind which produces satire with the quality of greatness. That is embodied in the satirist whose passions are released and let go by some intolerable sense of wrong. He is maddened by the sense of men being maddened; his tongue becomes an unruly member, and testifies against all mankind. Such a man was Swift...But neither did he laugh because he was unhappy, like Swift.

Man is more himself, man is more manlike, when joy is the fundamental thing in him, and grief the superficial. Melancholy should be an innocent interlude, a tender and fugitive frame of mind; praise should be the permanent pulsation of the soul. Pessimism is at best an emotional half-holiday; joy is the uproarious labour by which all things live.

There was something that He covered constantly by abrupt silence or impetuous isolation. There was some one thing that was too great for God to show us when He walked upon our earth; and I have sometimes fancied that it was His mirth.

Suffice it to say here that the only serious reason which I can imagine inducing any one person to listen to any other is, that the first person looks to the second person with an ardent faith and a fixed attention, expecting him to say what he does not expect him to say. It may be a paradox, but that is because paradoxes are true. It may not be rational, but that is because rationalism is wrong. But clearly it is quite true that whenever we go to hear a prophet or teacher we may or may not expect wit, we may or may not expect eloquence, but we do expect what we do not expect. We may not expect the true, we may not even expect the wise, but we do expect the unexpected. If we do not expect the unexpected, why do we go there at all? If we expect the expected, why do we not sit at home and expect it by ourselves.

It is in vain for him to say that he is not quarrelling with the importation of humour into the controversy. He ought himself to be importing humour into every controversy; for unless a man is in part a humorist, he is only in part a man.

Kingsley Amis

BUTT: IT AIN'T ENOUGH

Laughter is evoked through comedy, comedy through surprise, and surprise through the depiction of humorous juxtapositions. Kingsley Amis's *That Uncertain Feeling* features John Lewis, a man whose adulterous escapade with Mrs. Elizabeth Gruffyd-Williams teaches him profound existential lessons on lust, love, and life. Butt: Amis knew, in order to get his readers smiling, this was not enough. Merely to describe how a penurious twenty-six-year-old married librarian with moth-eaten clothing, no money for groceries, and an indefatigable toddler at home might betray some interest in a wealthy, beautiful woman's sudden and boisterous advances would be obvious. But Amis wrote comedy, and comedy relies on surprise; therefore, in the pursuit of great comedy, Amis chose to juxtapose in two ways. Firstly, he juxtaposed the novel's scenes of literary solemnity against scenes of irreverent slapstick. Secondly, he mirrored that pattern in Lewis's language, juxtaposing the loose, slang-ridden recalcitrance of a Breezy narration style against a euphemistically understated narrative style.

John Lewis is a young, disgruntled proletarian with militant feelings towards the wealthy Bourgeoise; he is also a scholar of Welsh literature and something of a pedant; he could be construed as what some people refer to today as a broke-ass snob. In this way, it only makes sense that Lewis's language be so interestingly humorous, carrying with it both the Holden Caufield-esque eye-spitting of the Breezy narration style that bobbysoxers and undergraduates alike seem to love and enjoy, and the wit-riddled irony of an understated, Dickensian-esque narration style favored by those with chronic dyspepsia.

Strunk and White told us never to affect a "breezy manner," as it reveals "the work of an egocentric, the person who imagines that everything that comes to mind is of general interest and that uninhibited prose creates high spirits and carries the day." A breezy manner is a kind of "alumni magazine," talk that wounds the more honorable amongst us. Consider three-hundred pages of the following: "Well, guys, here I am again dishing the dirt about your disorderly classmates, after pa$$ing a weekend in the Big Apple..." A difficult task, to be sure.

Although Mr. Strunk and Mr. White have doubtlessly slugged this unbearable archetype of the lexical narcissist on the chin, the gentlemen did not malign the use of a breezy manner in judicious conjunction with a more formal, understated one. And it was this concoction Amis thought worthy of two hundred and fifty-four pages.

We begin with the breezy when Lewis abbreviates linoleum floor as "Lino," whilst further describing the floors of the library by stating that "the place was starting to empty, thank God." An onslaught of informality: the library becomes an ambiguous pejorative noun, the imperfect past tense is employed, and the idea is punctuated by thanking the main Judeo-Christian deity for Lewis's triumph of Sloth. This narration, however, is juxtaposed but only a few sentences later with a creative euphemism as regards Lewis's inspection of a young woman's lower musculature: "Distraction was at hand: a female student from the local University College crossed my path some yards ahead and my glance dropped involuntarily to her legs." More chivalrous understatements have likely occurred in literature, but this usage is attractively subtle in the way it follows Lewis's cocksure breeziness with the formal admission that his eyes were not voluntarily under his control, that in some way he suffers tyranny. This continues throughout the novel. A man experiencing valid emotion and thus crying is "turn(ing) liquid eyes on [Lewis]," which is followed by lengthy, elaborate similes and metaphors anent the uncertain feeling of following another man's wife who has just then offered up her body up to his discretion: "We moved together towards the entrance-hall. I felt I was swinging in an absurdly unnatural way, like a schoolboy on stage for the first time in his life. Did I always swing my arms as if I were carrying a pair of empty buckets? Surely not. And what did I suppose I was going to say next?" Humorous language, Amis knew, is only half the battle; therefore, he also knew that, to write a humorous novel, one must also depict humorous scenes.

It is funny to watch other people suffer. The Germans, recent history suggests, are particularly fond of this notion, and even have a word for it called *Schadenfreude,* which most literally translates to disappointment-joy. A similar logic applies to Amis's juxtaposition of solemn, unironic narrative against humorous relief. This heightens the humor, as a narrative saturated in only the sugary treacle of the cutely ironic becomes cloying and indeed a real bellyache to read. This release from solemnity to comedy produces a kind of joy in the reader, suggesting that the dark times are never without something to smile about.

Consider the case of Lewis's suspicions that his wife and a failed playwright named Probert are having an affair: "I looked around for Jean. Probert was talking hard to her, with Elizabeth listening rather attentively. She caught my glance and mouthed some phrase at me, pointing to Probert. No thanks, I thought; whatever it is, no thanks. I smiled and waved to her, then hurried out." Now consider the sentence immediately thereafter: "it was wonderful in the lavatory." His wife's flirting with an unattractive literary imposter turns into supreme bathroom bliss.

Further consider Lewis's leading of his mistress down a poorly lit alleyway, in which "[he] stumble(s) on something soft, a bundle of washing or corpse, and warned her about it," whereupon Mrs. Davies, a nettlesome neighbor, calls into the darkness, inquiring into whether it might be her husband or son walking that same alley. Lewis continues the narrative: "ignoring this, I began climbing the stairs..." Examples of this quick shift from the solemn to the humorous may be gleaned from about every single page in the novel.

Yet, this formula, and it is indeed a kind of formula, somehow never gets old, never flags, never tires. This is due to the contrivance of a *truly* surprising juxtaposition; if it is *truly* surprising and *truly* a juxtaposition, by definition, it will work every single time. Recall the last time someone said that they just did not feel like laughing that day. That person was a fool. Laughter is not a choice. It is a visceral reaction, a reaction caused by surprise, and surprise *is* enough.

Charles Dickens

THE IMPORTANCE OF THE UNNECESSARY

Why, whenever one failed poet in brown corduroy asks another yawning novelist on hiatus what his favorite literary epoch is, does that same overweight adjunct professor, after briefly considering the state of contemporary options, always respond with "the nineteenth century"? The nineteenth century was the heyday of the novel—the heyday of Realism and the lavish, unnecessary detail. It is likely this truth that forces that very same part-time bike courier to respond with the century aforementioned. Good Realist writers were and are concerned with (un)necessary details. And it seems to be the unnecessary, and not the necessary, that reminds us of our world.

The Description is a lost art. And the description has received this predicate nominative adjectival pejoration due to our present unhealthy obsession with The Useful, The Economic, and The Necessary. According to James Wood's *How Fiction Works,* the nineteenth century was the renaissance of the unnecessary detail:

"19th-century realism...creates such an abundance of detail...that it will always contain a certain superfluidity, a built-in redundancy, that will *carry more detail than it needs*. In other words, fiction builds into itself a lot of surplus detail just as life is full of surplus detail." Charles Dickens's *The Posthumous Papers of the Pickwick Club*, written and serialized beginning in 1836, is not only a detail-besotted, post-doctorate-level, mirth-driven abdominal workout, but it is also an A-1 exercise in The Unnecessary.

Dickens was fond of publishing an instant Classic every other year of his life. It gave him something of a thrill, it is supposed. It is, however, his first novel, *The Pickwick Papers*, that has been praised by many an above-average citizen as quite possibly his best work. Not yet a quarter of a century old, Dickens was, according to master essayist and competent fiction writer G.K. Chesterton, "in the youthful whirl of the kind of world he would like to create." The scrapbook-like style of *The Pickwick Papers* attempts to tell twenty stories at once, out of which a nameless and elemental ecstasy emanates from a young man in mid-season stride at the kind of thing that he does best: witty humor.

Yet, one cannot begin to report reliably on nameless elements of ecstasy without first reporting on Dickens's gift for description, as, for Dickens, these two concepts are tightly intertwined.

Firstly, gather all your friends who are fluent in Ancient Greek. Now, gather all your friends who are fluent in Latin. Very good. Now that you are still alone and with quite a bit of free time on your hands, this might be a great time to ponder on the fact that the average sentence-length, from the time of Shakespeare to today, has decreased over seventy-five percent, from over seventy words per sentence to under fifteen. A much-needed decrease in convoluted thinking, some might say. A woeful increase in small ideas, other would riposte. Either way, it remains true that we use fewer words than ever to describe our world.

In the days before divorce and UberEATS, there was a thing called a Classical Education, whose interests were, briefly stated, to bestow onto its students a rich and fulfilling connection with the roots of human civilization and a meaningful, unfractured perspective of the world. Students in the nineteenth century were ensconced in this education. More pertinently, a Classical Education is well-versed in Ancient Greek and Latin, languages saturated with the long sentence, or *hypotaxis.*

They say that brevity is the soul of wit. This is a hoax of the highest order. Hypotaxis enjoys many long-since-forgotten philological entreaties; it is sexy: we inherently like to strip away its layers of meaning and tease our mental faculties with its hidden parts. A well-constructed bout of hypotaxis is also scintillatingly complex and gains the reader's trust, as it verifies that the author has thought a goodish deal about what he is saying. Try to convince an editor today to publish an opening sentence like that of *The Pickwick Papers*:

> *The first ray of light which illumines the gloom, and converts into a dazzling brilliancy that obscurity in which the earlier history of the public career of the immortal Pickwick would appear to be involved, is derived from the perusal of the following entry in the Transactions of the Pickwick Club, which the editor of these papers feels the highest pleasure in laying before his readers, as a proof of the careful attention, indefatigable assiduity, and nice discrimination, with which his search among the multifarious documents confided to him has been conducted.*

Here, Dickens reminds modern readers of the comma, the dependent clause, and the relative clause—all important elements for a well-scribbled bit of hypotaxis—each of which serve to render cleaner, more deliberate transitions, and therefore stronger, more discrete ideas, as well-placed clauses and commas show a clear mind discriminating in an intelligent fashion.

Moreover, humor already begins to run its long nose interestedly along the fence. This is due to the above's lengthy description for a simple process. The narrator could have written, "once upon a time in England" and collected a similar paycheck. But Dickens was made of better stuff. He knew that, if one would like to make something funny, then a good rule of thumb is to defy expectation. Therefore, in humorous writing, it is a fine idea to consider judiciously extending passages whose existence could otherwise be missed with a sneeze. And, if one is able to add irony to that uniquely elongated passage, then one really has nothing at which one may sneeze. For this latest suggestion, let us return to understatement, which was briefly touched upon in our section on Jerome K. Jerome.

To elaborate further on this wonderful rhetorical trope, understatement is whenever one writes something worthy of exclamation in a calm, tactful register, whilst employing euphemisms and questing after impossible feats of decorousness. This greatly increases the humor, as understatement increases the distance and tension in such a fashion that a kind of subtle absurdity takes place. A few examples might include the following:

- Her sweaters do not exactly promote the full range of the diaphragm.

- That part of town has not quite yet felt the positive effects of gentrification.
- Her appearance performed curious feats upon his libido.
- A gunshot in close quarters is a sound of some concern.
- I consider the reports of my death to be exaggerated.

A heated horse chase through the English countryside to capture a homeless con artist

who shanghaied an aristocrat's middle-aged daughter with the prospect of marrying her in order to help bolster the English economy with broadminded ideas of her fortune are also not immune to such rhetorical arrangements:

> *The horses in the first chaise started on at their utmost speed; and those in Mr Wardle's galloped furiously behind them.*
>
> *'I see his head,' exclaimed the choleric man, 'Damme, I see his head.'*
>
> *'So do I," said Mr Pickwick, 'that's he.'*
>
> *Mr Pickwick was not mistaken. The countenance of Mr Jingle, completely coated with the mud thrown up by the wheels, was plainly discernable at the window of his chaise; and the motion of his arm, which he was waving violently towards the postilions, denoted that he was encouraging them to increase exertion.*
>
> *The interest was intense.*

Interest? Why not hatred, anger, or the flaming passion of justice? Because those would not be witty. Also, a special redundancy occurs with the word "intense." Together, this understatement leaves the reader smiling at the fact that so much was obvious, and one's gently tickled fancy invests itself in the details of the image with great interest.

One may similarly think of understatement as writing something as one would a legal report or medical document. Police, lawyers, and doctors must try to report coolly and objectively on what are often less than ordinary occurrences, some of which are truly ludicrous. The result is that some of these reports read with supreme comedy.

Consider, for instance, this recollection of a sudden dust-up that occurs with the Pickwickians in Ipswich whilst being carted away by local police:

> *'Stand back,' said the outraged Mr Grummer. By way of adding force to the command, he thrust the brass emblem of royalty into Sam's neckcloth with one hand, and seized Sam's collar with the other, a compliment which Mr Weller returned by knock(ing) him down out of hand, having previously, with the utmost consideration, knocked down a chairman for him to lie upon.*
>
> *Whether Mr Winkle was seized with a temporary attack of that species of insanity which originates in a sense of injury, or animated by this display of Mr Weller's valor, is uncertain; but certain is, that he no sooner saw Mr Grummer fall, than he made terrific onslaught on a small boy who stood next to him; whereupon Mr Snodgrass, in a truly christian spirit, and in order that he might take no one unawares, announced in a very loud tone that he was going to begin, and proceeded to take off his coat with the*

utmost deliberation. He was immediately surrounded and secured.

Written in an elevated, utterly enjoyable legalese style, the passage does not report that Mr Grummer forcefully detains Samuel Weller and threatens to crack his skull with his ornate police baton, rather "compliment(s)" him with "the brass emblem of royalty." Samuel Weller does not fight back, rather he returns the compliment, "...with the utmost consideration, [having] knocked down a chairman for (Mr Grummer) to lie upon." Additionally, Mr Snodgrass was not tackled, beaten, and arrested, rather "surrounded and secured." Notice as well that legalese bodes well with archaic where-compounds, such as *wherefrom, whereof,* or, in this case, the gentle *whereupon.* Where-compounds are a great transitional choice of the Wit interested in conveying a descriptive bout of hypotaxis with a certain pedantic humor.

Perhaps someone whom you know has rather liberal notions towards the idea of The Calorie and has been offered, on occasion, less than flattering commentary thereabout; perhaps it sounded something much like what Jingle, the aforementioned homeless con artist, offered to Mr Tupman, the most corpulent Pickwickian member: "'Rather fat—grown up Bacchus—cut the leaves—dismounted from the tub, and adopted kersey, eh?—not double distilled, but double milled—ha! ha!—pass the wine.'"

This is a charge of some brazenness. Mr Tupman, however, takes the high road and decides on understatement, with a dash of hypotaxis:

Whether Mr Tupman was somewhat indignant at the peremptory tone in which he was desired to pass the wine

> *which the stranger passed so quickly away; or whether he felt very properly scandalized, at an influential member of the Pickwick Club being ignominiously compared to a dismounted Bacchus, is a fact not yet completely ascertained. He passed the wine, coughed twice, and looked at the stranger for several seconds with a stern intensity.*

Though a common misconception and favorite mantra of a jealous minimalist the world over, Charles Dickens was not paid by the word, rather by installment. He does have one enviable up on us twenty-first century lexoslaves, however, in that he was paid. Nevertheless, no matter how one might like to spin Dickens's preternatural ability to describe at length any and all things as merely a by-the-word, middle-brow money laundering scheme, the fact remains that the gentleman could indeed describe. The opposite is, on the other hand, also true. One may, with rather a good conscience, say that Dickens could equally disguise himself as a man of some lexical economy. One of his favorite tools for achieving this end is *syllepsis.*

Syllepsis is a rhetorical scheme, in which a single verb is used to describe several actions that occur thereafter, most often in the form of a series, or list. For example, Mr Pickwick and his friends were not introduced to the ladies and then introduced to their dinner, rather they were "introduced to the ladies and soon afterwards their dinner." One might presume that Miss Bolo went straight home in a flood of tears and soon after that found a sedan-chair, on which she continued to wax most lachrymose. Miss Bolo, the clever gal she is, instead "went straight home, in a flood of tears and a sedan-chair." Such a display of double-x energy might lead some to procure their hats and then find a dryer way out of there.

A better way, Dickens would suggest, would be if one "took his hat, and his leave" simultaneously, saving both time and the reader's finer sensibilities.

In effect, syllepsis performs the opposite duty of the above-described tactics employed to lengthen a description of a mundane event; it cuts out all of the hoopla and melds everything into one moving image. The best way to write a knee-slapping syllepsis is to construct a combination of unlikely parts that, after reading to the end of the sentence, paradoxically prove a pattern of incontrovertible naturalness.

The truth at the heart of the matter is that Dickens, as all great thinkers are, was a man of patterns. And perhaps one of the most readily decipherable patterns in Dickens's writing is his obsession for parallelism, a technique first mentioned during our ride-along with Twain. For one of the better Resisting Arrest charges recorded at the sentence level, let us return to the Pickwickians' sporting mix-up with Ipswich's finest:

> *Violent was Mr. Weller's indignation as he was borne along; numerous were the allusions to the personal appearance and demeanor of Mr. Grummer and his companion; and valorous were the defiances to any six of the gentlemen present, in which he vented his dissatisfaction.*

To connote an interconnectedness of meaning, everything is nicely tied together with semicolons, an element of punctuation in today's world almost as extinct as parallelism. Semicolons connect two independent clauses that are—or, more subtly, one would like to be—highly related in meaning. In this case, the semicolons show the actions of the Pickwickians to be done in a kind of solidarity.

Additionally, adjectives lead each independent clause, suggesting that "violent...numerous...[and] valorous" should be recognized as one animated and functioning image. Neither does it hurt that Dickens paired the words "numerous" and "valorous," which share identical suffixes, thus doing the human ear a bit of good.

A slightly more grammatically orthodox version of parallelism, the following example hardly deviates in pattern-sequence: "...the London coach deposited Mr Weller senior at the door, his legs deposited him in the bar, and his eyes showed him his son." This kind of tightly written parallelism renders a quick shot-to-shot feeling. Dickens's choice of Mr Weller senior's legs and eyes as the chief actors in each respective line also affords the mind's eye a close-up, zoomed-in effect worthy of a turned lip and appreciative nod.

Then we have a classic farcical parallelism. You have seen it before in physical comedy: That Guy looks at Someone, Someone looks at What's-His-Name, and What's-His-Name looks at the Other Guy. More often than not, it ends with their all looking at each other. Or, with a bit more oomph: "The magistrate looked at Mr Jinks, Mr Jinks looked at the magistrate, and officers looked at each other in amazement." Best employed during embarrassing or otherwise tension-filled moments, this writerly tactic aids in the feeling that time has slowed down and conjures the illusion that each person beheld the other with great pause and moment.

As perhaps noticed, it is also not a bad idea to make what is parallel occur three times. Despite tough competition from seven and forty, three reigns undisputedly supreme as the most sacred number in print. But Dickens proved that his holy trinity could, on occasion, be dissented: "...the chairman <u>trotting</u>, the prisoners <u>following</u>, Mr Pickwick <u>oratorizing</u>, and the crowd <u>shouting</u>."

The present continuous verb at the end of each phrase is the most important word of each, and having the most important image at the end of a sentence is called *rearrangement*. Rearrangement may consist of an emphatic word, a pun, or, best of all, a clever image. As the end of the sentence is the part of the sentence that people remember the most, it is a good idea to leave a lasting impression by slapping on it the patterned nylon stockings.

It is important to note that contrast helps people see things better. If it be one's intention to lighten the white of a drawing without adding more white, then just add black. The same goes for writing symmetry. Symmetry adds a bit more backswing to its biff whenever contrasted against "loose" sentences, sentences that have minimal shape or rhetorical flourish. But the truest Wit, it must be said, writes no loose sentences. Loose sentences are to him redolent of Sarah's thoughts whenever Abraham arrived twiddling his thumbs and talking about becoming the mother of nations: inconceivable. Under the guise of something subtle should lie in wait sentences of sundry deliberate patterns that, whenever side-by-side, ready effortlessly and naturally.

But even the best prose writers must deign themselves to a bit of dialogue now and then. It *is* conceivable that Dickens even enjoyed writing dialogue, judging by the amount of it in his writings. Better still, he had a lovely, little knack of juxtaposing his high-register, understated narratives with sudden jerks dialogue that rip readers out of their trance and leave them squawking ignominiously out of the library.

Mr Pickwick sets out upon his journey with mystical placidity. With the completion of only the first few pages of the book, he has already meditated philosophically upon mankind, deemed it good, and boarded a coach with all the deepest goodwill, infatuated with an unconditional love for all creatures great and small. Whenever such moods strike, elusive as they are, one feels a quick chat-up with the nearest stranger an event as natural as a soft rain on a lazy April afternoon. Mr Pickwick follows this fancy thusly, asking the driver,

> *'How old is that horse, my friend?' enquired Mr Pickwick, rubbing his nose with the shilling he had reserved for the fare.*
>
> *'Forty-two,' replied the driver, eyeing him askant.*
>
> *'What!' ejaculated Pickwick.*

Modern readers will find some additional mirth with the final attribution describing Mr Pickwick's ejaculation. As regards the more pertinent prospect of retirement, horses hold more eager views than humans, entering their mid-twenties with their eyes on the prize. Mr Pickwick's reaction reminds us of that fact. And the fact is that surprising dialogue-juxtapositions in *The Pickwick Papers* are standing around every corner with a wrench, and you owe them money.

Just consider the remainder of the coachman's scene:

> *'Here's your fare,' said Mr Pickwick, holding out the shilling to the driver.*
>
> *What was the learned man's astonishment, when that unaccountable person flung the money on the pavement, and requested in figurative terms to be allowed the pleasure of fighting him (Mr Pickwick) for the amount.*
>
> *'You're mad,' said Mr Snodgrass.*
>
> *'Or drunk,' said Mr Winkle.*

'Or both,' said Mr Tupman.

'Come on,' said the cab-driver, sparring away like clock-work. 'come one—all four on you."

Then, Sam the Cabman, after an impressive combination upon Mr Pickwick's person and putting in some diligent work on both Mr Snodgrass and Mr. Tupman, finally "dashed the whole temporary supply of breath out of Winkle's body..."

Smartly composed scenes written well enough for finishing school juxtaposed against scenes of violence perpetrated against old men and fops never cease to please. Dickens then reads the reader's mind with a bit of mid-fight meta-commentary with the aptly timed, "what's the fun?" followed by the image of a "rather tall thin young man in a green coat emerging suddenly from the coachyard", whom we later learn to be the charlatan Jingle and thus the true start of the novel.

Just moments later, that same perceived gentleman recounts the following tale during a leisurely country coach-ride with the Pickwickians: "'...five children—mother—tall lady, eating sandwiches—forgot about the arch—crash—knock—children look around—mother's head off—sandwich in her hand...'" Notwithstanding antic tales of headless mothers, Jingle's helping the Pickwickians during the heated boxing imbroglio is so verily appreciated that the gang decides to invite the newcomer to dinner and drinks at their destination of Kent. And it was during this browsing and sluicing when Jingle invites Mr Tupman to a Kentish party promised to exceed all others, which is only moments before Jingle describes Tupman as a dismounted Bacchus.

A homeless swindler of low repute, Jingle had not a coat to wear to the ball, so Tupman offers him Mr Winkle's coat, a unique blue coat with brass buttons engraved with the likeness of Mr Pickwick. Whilst at the party, Jingle insults an apparently important military doctor, Doctor Slammer, who sends a lacky the next morning to find the owner of the unique blue coat with the strangely engraved brass buttons. The owner of said coat was found and subsequently challenged to a duel.

One intestine-altering afternoon later and Mr Winkle arrives shakingly to the duel—against a shockingly cool, almost bored-looking military veteran—uncertain of how to load a pistol. Just before Slammer ends Mr Winkle's existence, he stops and proclaims that Winkle is not the man who had insulted him the night prior. "I am not the person. I know it," ejaculated Mr Winkle in return.

It is during this tense moment that a flatulent butterknife is slid greasily into the atmosphere of the scene by way of commentary from one of Doctor Slammer's posse, a man sitting on a camp stool who goes by the name of Payne and who wanted, above all else, satisfaction: "' Then, that,'" said the man with the camp stool, "'is an affront to Doctor Slammer, and sufficient reason for proceeding.'" Doctor Slammer heeds this statement not, whereupon the man with the camp stool continues: "'Unless,'" interposed the man with the camp-stool, "'unless Mr Winkle feels himself aggrieved by the challenge; in which case, I submit, he has a right to satisfaction.'" At this, Mr Winkle expresses himself to be quite satisfied already. The diligent spectator, however, offers further solutions: "'Or possibly,'" said the man with the camp-stool, "the gentleman's second may feel himself affronted with some observations which fell from me at an earlier period of this meeting: if so, I shall be happy to give *him* satisfaction immediately.'"

Indeed, perhaps one of the key elements to this duel-scene is that Mr Winkle—The Pickwick Club's alleged sportsman, equestrian, and sharpshooter—cannot fight, ride a horse, or shoot a gun. And this concept it important throughout the entirety of *The Pickwick Papers.* Dickens achieves perfect physical comedy and excellent dramatic irony in his scenes through the creation of comical *caricatures,* a great method of exploiting human foibles and foolishness. Mr Winkle's knowledge on the topic of firearms provides, indeed, more than one instance of entertainment for the reader:

> *'Now, Mr. Winkle,' said the host, reloading his own gun. 'Fire away.'*
>
> *Mr. Winkle advanced, and levelled his gun. Mr. Pickwick and his friends cowered involuntarily to escape damage from the heavy fall of rooks, which they felt quite certain would be occasioned by the devastating barrel of their friend. There was a solemn pause—a shout—a flapping of wings—a faint click.*
>
> *'Hollo!' said the old gentleman.*
>
> *'Won't it go?' inquired Mr. Pickwick.*
>
> *'Missed fire,' ssid Mr. Winkle, who was very pale—probably from disappointment.*
>
> *'Odd,' said the old gentleman, taking the gun. 'Never knew one of them miss fire before. Why, I don't see anything of the cap.'*
>
> *Bless my soul!' said Mr. Winkle, 'I declare I forgot the cap!'*
>
> *The slight omission was rectified. Mr. Pickwick crouched again. Mr. Winkle stepped forward with an air of*

> *determination and resolution; and Mr. Tupman looked out from behind a tree. The boy shouted; four birds flew out. Mr. Winkle fired. There was a scream as of an individual—not a rook—in corporal anguish. Mr. Tupman had saved the lives of innumerable unoffending birds by receiving a portion of the charge in his left arm.*

In fact, the descriptions of Mr Winkle's impressive feats of gun-bungling is something of a leitmotif in the book. After having already shot Tupman just weeks prior, Winkle again displays his developed rifling etiquette whilst the Pickwickians attempt to enjoy a short hunt with a close friend, Mr Wardle.

> *'Hi, Juno, lass-hi, old girl; down, Daph, down,' said Wardle, caressing the dogs. 'Sir Geoffrey still in Scotland, of course, Martin?'*
>
> *The tall gamekeeper replied in the affirmative, and looked with some surprise from Mr. Winkle, who was holding his gun as if he wished his coat pocket to save him the trouble of pulling the trigger, to Mr. Tupman, who was holding his as if he was afraid of it—as there is no earthly reason to doubt he really was.*
>
> *'My friends are not much in the way of this sort of thing yet, Martin,' said Wardle, noticing the look. 'Live and learn, you know. They'll be good shots one of these days. I beg my friend Winkle's pardon, though; he has had some practice.'*
>
> *Mr. Winkle smiled feebly over his blue neckerchief in acknowledgment of the compliment, and got himself so mysteriously entangled with his gun, in his modest confusion,*

that if the piece had been loaded, he must inevitably have shot himself dead upon the spot.

'You mustn't handle your piece in that 'ere way, when you come to have the charge in it, Sir,' said the tall gamekeeper gruffly; 'or I'm damned if you won't make cold meat of some on us.'

Mr. Winkle, thus admonished, abruptly altered his position, and in so doing, contrived to bring the barrel into pretty smart contact with Mr. Weller's head.

'Hollo!' said Sam, picking up his hat, which had been knocked off, and rubbing his temple. 'Hollo, sir! if you comes it this vay, you'll fill one o' them bags, and something to spare, at one fire.'

Here the leather-legginged boy laughed very heartily, and then tried to look as if it was somebody else, whereat Mr. Winkle frowned majestically.

And Mr Tupman, who is loosely portrayed as something of a master of chivalry, proceeds to ogle at some women, leer at others, and, with supernatural interest, submit requests into the whereabouts of still others. To begin the dossier, it would not be a mistake to return to the aforementioned countryside ride with Jingle. In the span of but a page, Tupman's defect is made clear:

'Fine girl, Sir' (to Mr Tracy Tupman, who had been bestowing sundry anti-pickwickian glances on a young lady by the road side).

'Very!' said Mr Tupman.

'...You have been to Spain, Sir?' inquired Mr TracyTupman. 'Many conquests, Sir?' inquired Mr Tupman.

> *(With regard to Jingle's alleged former lover, Donna Christiana, and his having her stomach pump in his portmanteau)...'Is the lady in England now, Sir?'*
>
> *'Dead, Sir—dead'... Mr Tupman said nothing; but he thought of Donna Christiana, the stomach pump...and his eyes filled with tears.*

Not long thereafter, at their dinner together, Mr Tupman evinces his chief concern of the evening:

> *'Many fine women in this town, do you know, Sir?' inquired Mr Tupman, with great interest.*
>
> *...'I should very much like to go,' said Tupman, resuming the subject of the ball, 'very much.'*
>
> *...The wine was passed, and a fresh supply ordered. The visitor talked, the Pickwickians listened. Mr Tupman felt every moment more disposed for the ball...'How I should like to go,' said Tupman, again,*
>
> *...The temptation to be present at the ball, and to form his first impression of the beauty of the Kentish ladies, was strong upon Mr Tupman.*

And, when having arrived at the ball: *charming women.*

Doing accurate impressions of others is funny. Think of your favorite wisecrack. Whenever he is telling a story, does he vary his voice? Does he carry the same voice throughout? Or, does he change accents and syntactical patterns, use queer words, and refer or allude to the things to which each character or caricature would refer and allude to in his own locality, culture, or general experience.

Contrary to the guild of humorless academics who admonish otherwise, accurate impressions suggest not a malicious attack on another's identity or assert some nebulous idea of supremacy. Quite the contrary.

Many decades ago, there was a thing called a Sense of Humor, which believe it or not, could be used by and applied to everyone. Emulation, the sages have said, is the sincerest form of flattery and to perfect this emulation is to show deep affection. The person who does accurate impressions of others has spent a lot of time thinking about other people and has subsequently learned a great deal about their condition as human beings; he who performs excellent impressions has taken time to truly learn something specific about the subject, be they gestures, accents, or cultural expectations—bringing all involved that much closer to understanding the human condition.

This was not lost on Dickens. Indeed, the astute reader of these pages will have already deduced Mr Weller's not inconsiderable contributions on the matter. Mr Weller's appearance in the part on caricature displayed something in his speech that is preached against by all halfwit MFA programs and publishers alike: dialect.

Cockneys of the nineteenth century must have missed the lecture on dialect's being an assault on their identity, for they were not at all offended by Weller's lexical eccentricities. They saw themselves in the character. And they loved it. The sales of *The Pickwick Papers* grew exponentially upon Weller's appearance in the novel. Cockneys liked to see in print a character that truly represented them—talked how they talked, thought how they thought, laughed how they laughed.

An avid admirer of *The Pickwick Papers*, G.K. Chesterton had this to say about the humor of the English poor and its connection to Samuel Weller:

> *The English poor live in an atmosphere of humor. Irony is the very air that they breathe...the phrase that leaps to their lips is the ironical phrase. I remember once being driven in a hansom cab down a street that turned out to be a cul de sac, and brought us bang up against a wall. The driver and I simultaneously said something. But I said: "This'll never do!" and he said: "This is all right!"...*
>
> *Many comic writers had described the clever rascal and his ridiculous dupe; but here, in a fresh and very human atmosphere, we have a clever student who was not a rascal and a dupe who was not ridiculous. Sam Weller stands in some ways for a cheerful knowledge of the world; Mr. Pickwick stands for a still more cheerful ignorance of the world...Knowledge should be the servant and innocence the master.*

Samuel Weller, though a trifle inclined to truculence, drink, and illiteracy, is nonetheless the wittiest character in the book, conjuring as he did limitless unique images and lexical combinations during what Chesterton called his "incessant stream(s) of sane nonsense." These perceived paroxysms of idiocy have a definition in the real world: Wellerisms. Wellerisms are much like an analogy in that they depict a kind of comparison between two unlike situations that paint an image of slanted likeness in meaning. Take a long and sustained pull from the bottle of the forthcoming:

- *Out vith it, as the father said to his child, when he swallowed a farden.*
- *Now, gen'l'm'n, "fall on," as the English said to the French when they fixed bagginets*
- *All good feelin', sir – the wery best intentions, as the gen'l'm'n said ven he run away from his wife 'cos she seemed unhappy with him.*

Oscar Wilde reminded us that "we can forgive a man for making a useful thing as long as he does not admire it. The only excuse for making a useless thing is that one admires it intensely. All art is quite useless." Dialect and Wellerisms are gloriously unnecessary things. And, with that, I leave you with a wish by proxy:

> *Wery glad to see you, indeed, and hope our acquaintance may be a long 'un, as the gen'l'm'n said to the fi' pun' note.*

www.ingramcontent.com/pod-product-compliance
Lightning Source LLC
Chambersburg PA
CBHW020442160726
48196CB00081B/37

* 9 7 9 8 3 3 0 2 9 1 0 9 0 *